The Burns Unit

Nina Ines Ward

Flirtation #11

salò press

All poems are original to this collection

978-1-8383602-1-4

Printed and Bound by 4Edge

Cover design and layout by Salò Press

Typeset by Sophie Essex

Published by:
Salò Press
85 Gertrude Road
Norwich
UK

editorsalòpress@gmail.com
www.salòpress.com

for Molly Ellen Pearson

Contents

(i)

no one remembers
what they eat at funerals
no one remembers
my body on the table
only my head between my hands

we will all be cooked
our flesh will rest
we will taste
our own marinade
before anyone else
we will all be cooked
so keep checking to see
how far along you are

(ii)

it gave me bad history, like a salmon
going back to the wrong stream. they wheeled
me to the burns unit, i wasn't
even peeling yet. my house caught fire
last year, but i started coughing
yesterday. my throat like an overhead
hanger, he liked the extra space.
my throat is the river i am trying to
get back to. no one gives
a number for my injury, yet.
it's to prevent victim mentality.
someone explains:
if you get told you're burning
then you start to act like it.

(iii)

yesterday my neighbour harvested
the loose scales of my skin
to be close to what sucks you all in, they said.
i'm still waiting for visitors but they disappoint me
like a vitamin deficiency.
i can only hear a crackle on the phone
but i nod like i'm part of something.
been dreaming inside the house
he is always there
mouth open, walking from room to room.
jammed in his tongue, my key
will never budge. something crawling
around the metal.

(iv)

i sit like a petri dish, everyone is waiting
to see what will grow. some place
bets on the innovation of my flesh:
where do you think it will hurt?
we all go through the motions of healing
crutches & bandages.
it's best to start before we know what's gone wrong.
last night this whole body started lactating;
my sheets were damp, i had to suck them dry.
now they wring me out over a bucket
twice a day, creased hands moving
over the damp shelves of my body.
i leave myself open for them, every morning
like a fridge that wants to be touched.

(v)

everyone burns when they sleep.
i listen to the rustle of spoilt
meat. whisper into the receiver,
there's no one in the other rooms.
the plastic relaxes around my ear, softens
in my hand. *i'm a good person.* i listen,
a tongue clicks louder & harder:
you're bad, you're bad, you're bad...
i hang up, my ear dressed
with spit. cold white fat
wedged underneath my fingernails.

(vi)
after molly ellen pearson

what will happen to you
if the rats stop moving?
my new friend has the most dazzling affliction
i couldn't tell if it was inside or crawling on the surface
sometimes if i'm lucky i see one,
porous lump of flesh and tail
they have no eyes, they have no face
i hear their muffled voices
they light up at night & speed
around the body like toy race cars
it's easy to get jealous of the rat city
my new friend stopped talking weeks ago
what will happen to you
if the rats never stop?

(vii)
from *temptation*, new order.

o you've got green mouth:
i kiss the edges, young tissue
falls away like landslide.
o you've got blue mouth:
my tongue, the lemon juicer
on the kitchen surface.
my tongue, the lemon juicer
sticky with healing.
o you've got grey mouth:
anything beyond the wound is senseless.
everything is numb, except the openings.

(viii)
after x

i have a dream where we hold hands
walking down into the belly of the rat king
it always rains
waist deep in the stew
my heart like a fontanelle
would be nice to stay

my house in the river is still on fire

(ix)

it is only appropriate to swallow:
saliva, melted molars, splinters
of charred bone.
honestly, i've never felt better.
when a priest offers up mutton
i smile, spit out half a tonsil into his hand
& open wide. *i'll have what she's having.*
my sad, strange meat can't find its expiration date.
there's no cure for my cure. i discover
different species of pain each day.
there's no cure for my cure.
some keep what the body can't hold
i consume it all.

(x)

it's awards night,
the girl with no holes
is applying a smile like sudocrem.
string music swells in the background like an abscess &
she recieves a trophy for *most improved attitude*.
the next day she is gone.
her holes came back for her in the night,
they couldn't remember the way home.
sorry, i heard them whisper as they
swallowed her fingers. *sorry, i never knew.*
all that was left of her was pellets, left alone
in her bed like orphaned eggs.

(xi)

the estate agent has curved hands like fins on a dinner plate. his shoes still wet from walking through the water. i ask, *what's happened to the house?* he lifts his hand to my face, *the fire has been moved to the garden. there are people already living there.* slowly, he picks away my oldest scabs & eats them. i take my tenancy papers while he chews. it's tricky maintaining a throat in flames, i don't even bleed, piss or shit anymore. everything is ash. at night, chimney sweepers take away my mess; their lungs baptized in my dust.

(xii)

each day exposes hope, new depths
of meat annunciate themselves to me with
porous wings & garbled voices.
they speak of the first burn.
they speak in heavy tongues throughout
the night, veins hot with godliness.
it will take months for me to understand.
how long until the wound begins to happen?
sleepwalking backwards in circles
to remember how i got here, a warm hole
presses itself firmly against the back of my head.

(xiii)

after x

in a dream i feed you pennies
until your eyes light up like two eclipses
every breath rings out across the meaty twilight
i sit on your stomach & the coins dig into my thighs
i am tender as a flu shot
open your mouth, let me look down
into your well with no one to pull me back.

(xiv)

after francesca kritikos

everyone must present an offering for
our lady of the turning eyes, it is customary.
at her smooth feet lay curls of burnt hair &
pus that never dries.
bloodied nails heaped in her cupped palms
like a harvest of gunky moons.
i look around my body for leftovers but
all the plates have been scraped clean.
pulling her face close to mine, i kiss her cheek
she tastes of salt & oil & her eyes are turning.
a single red tear rolls slowly down her face
like an incision, my tongue kneels at her altar.
i suck her blue rare eyes like a lamb, my tummy
bright & trembling until she smiles.

(xv)

after lawrence greenlee

when i wake up my neck is extinguished,
the river has begun to thaw.
at the end of my bed a rat stares at me   ·
you need to leave now, it whispers.
i walk over to the rat city
it is deserted, streets hollow
only filled with gusts of wind.
i wander across the hot tarmac for days, spitting
on sidewalks & listening to it fry in the heat.
in the road ahead, a monster hag-stone
unseals it's mouth like a sacred fire well. flames wrap
around my hands like damp cloth. yes, of course.

(xvi)

every word is a magic word, so when
i tell you this it will become real
& all the will doors open:

my dad holding the cake
tiny candles in his glasses

my eyes in ceiling, watching over
this growing stack of bodies

see the man lifting my arm
& then letting it drop

(xvii)

i exit the hag-stone one limb at a time, collapse
into a sharp soup of arms & legs.
weeks later, a crow comes along
puts me back together.
once breathing happens again i say,
" ███████████ "
it has no feathers, it's body is helpless
like the inside of a dried fig.
i carry it in my palms
follow the stream i was spawned from.
" ███████████ "
it hums in response, like a pacemaker
& i think i understand.

(xviii)

after callum browne

this is just a house now. the flames
in the garden don't mean anything.
when i go inside
there are no clocks, scales or cups.
in the kitchen i place the crow
into a bowl of royal jelly. it's stopped
but out of the eyes come primoses.
the others are here, they help me
dice red onions & plum tomatoes
while my meat marinates.
their voices like smoke signals in a glass jar.

Nina Ines Ward is a poet based in Brighton. Her work can be found online at *Seam Editions* and *Spam Zine*. She is a proud member of the Flat Earth Society and advocate for trepanation to be available through the NHS.

FIND YOUR POWER

CHAKRAS

An Hachette UK Company
www.hachette.co.uk

First published in Great Britain in 2023 by Godsfield,
an imprint of Octopus Publishing Group Ltd
Carmelite House, 50 Victoria Embankment, London EC4Y 0DZ
www.octopusbooks.co.uk

ISBN 978-1-8418-1549-7

A CIP catalogue record for this book is available from the British Library

Printed and bound in China

10 9 8 7 6 5 4 3 2 1

Publisher: Lucy Pessell
Designer: Isobel Platt
Editor: Feyi Oyesanya
Assistant Editor: Samina Rahman
Production Controller: Allison Gonsalves

Illustrations, all from Noun Project by Tricia Lara: Base Chakra on page 28 and 34, Sacral Chakra
on page 44 and 50, Solar Plexus on page 58 and 64, Heart Chakra on page 72 and 78, Throat
Chakra on page 86 and 92, Third Eye Chakra on page 100 and 105, and Crown Chakra on page 110
and 114.

This FSC® label means that materials used for the product have been responsibly sourced

FIND YOUR POWER

CHAKRAS

ROMOLA CARTER

GODSFIELD

CONTENTS

FIND
YOUR
POWER

When daily life becomes busy and your time and energy is pulled in many different directions, it can be difficult to find time to nourish yourself. Prioritizing your own wellbeing can be a struggle and you risk feeling overwhelmed, unsure of where to turn and what you need in order to feel lighter and find your inner strength.

Taking some time to focus on yourself, answering questions you may be avoiding or facing problems that are simmering away under the surface is the best gift you can give yourself. But it can be difficult to know where to start.

Sometimes all you need to learn life's big lessons is a little guidance. In this series of books you will learn about personal healing, and how to nourish your spirit. Explore practices which will help you to get clear on what you really want, and that will encourage you to

acknowledge – and deal with – any limiting beliefs or negative thoughts that might be holding you back in living life to your fullest power.

These books provide invaluable advice on how to create the best conditions for a healthier, happier, and more fulfilled life. Bursting with essential background, revealing insights and useful activities and exercises to enable you to understand and expand your personal practices every day, it's time to delve into your spiritual journey and truly Find Your Power.

Other titles in the series:

- *Find Your Power: Tarot*
- *Find Your Power: Manifest*
- *Find Your Power: Numerology*
- *Find Your Power: Runes*
- *Find Your Power: Crystals*
- *Find Your Power: Mindfulness*
- *Find Your Power: Meditation*

INTRODUCTION

Do you ever feel like things are somehow *off*, as if something in your life isn't quite as it should be, but you can't put your finger on exactly why? Sometimes, we might seem to have all the things we need – work, family, relationships, food, shelter – but still feel like something is off-kilter or out of balance. If this happens, we often look to external circumstances to try and find a solution, examining different things to see what's knocking us off course. But it's also important to turn our focus inwards and identify where things are out of balance within ourselves.

Learning about your chakras and how they work can be a meaningful and effective way to do this. Through understanding and connecting with your chakras and what they mean, you can gain a greater understanding and appreciation of your own needs, and learn different tools and techniques to bring things back into balance.

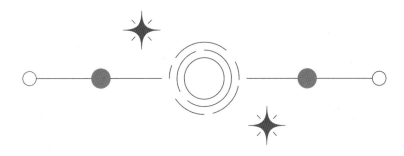

WHAT ARE CHAKRAS?

Each of us has a physical body that exists in the material world, but we also have a body of light, or subtle energy. This energy, sometimes known as *prana* or life force, flows through each of us, and connects with the physical body at key points known as chakras.

Chakra means 'wheel of light' in Sanskrit, and chakras can be imagined as spinning wheels that help provide a channel through which energy can flow in and out. It can help to imagine the flow of energy as a river and the chakras as water wheels along the river's path. If they are well-balanced, the water is able to flow smoothly and freely through the wheels, and the energy is directed to where it needs to go. If they are damaged or obstructed, the flow of the water can be blocked, and the energy cannot continue along its path. Similarly, if they are turning too fast, the flow of the water can spin out of control, becoming too fast and causing flooding and chaos.

Each chakra has a symbol known as a *yantra*: these are often some variation on the lotus flower, with different numbers of petals and other attributes.

ORIGINS AND HISTORY

The ideas we have about chakras today originate from the Sanskrit texts the *Upanishads*, part of the *Vedas* (ancient Hindu scriptures).

Chakras are also mentioned in some Buddhist traditions and play a role in *Kundalini* yoga. The concept has been developed and explored by various traditions over the years, and there are some fascinating historical and spiritual texts that explore their origins in great detail.

For the purposes of this book, we will be focusing on a Western understanding of the chakras developed by 20th-century thinkers and Theosophists, such as Sir John Woodroffe (whose 1919 book *The Serpent Power* helped to introduce the idea of chakras to the West) and Charles W. Leadbeater (whose 1927 book *The Chakras* was hugely influential on Western ideas about the chakras). To put it very simply, we will be looking at chakras as energy points connected with particular parts of the body and concerned with different issues and attributes.

In this sense, the chakras can be understood as a system for understanding and looking after your physical, emotional, intellectual and spiritual needs, and in so doing promoting a sense of balance and wellbeing.

Understanding and connecting with your chakras means you can gain a greater understanding of your own needs.

THE MAIN CHAKRAS

There are dozens if not hundreds of chakras, but in this book, we'll be focusing on the seven main chakras.

Each one is positioned at different points in the body, arranged vertically along the spine, from its base to the top of the head. The lower chakras are more concerned with the physical and material world, and the higher ones with the emotional, intellectual and spiritual.

Each chakra is associated with a particular colour and element, and each one focuses on a different aspect of our wellbeing. We'll look at each one in detail later in the book, but for now here is a brief overview.

THE ROOT CHAKRA, MULADHARA

It's red in colour, at the very base of the spine and related to the earth element.

The Root or Base Chakra is concerned with all things earthy and physical. This chakra is about our most essential physical survival needs, like food and shelter.

THE SACRAL CHAKRA, SVADHISTHANA

It's orange in colour, just below the navel and related to the water element.

The Sacral Chakra is concerned with physical and sensual pleasure and joy. This is about creativity, taking delight in the world around us, and connecting with others emotionally.

THE SOLAR PLEXUS CHAKRA, *MANIPURA*

Yellow in colour, this is located in the stomach, just above the navel and below the sternum. It's related to the fire element.

The Solar Plexus Chakra is concerned with power and purpose. It's about self-confidence and motivation, making plans and having a sense of focus and control.

THE HEART CHAKRA, *ANAHATA*

Green in colour, this is located in centre of the chest. It's related to the air element.

The Heart Chakra, as its name suggests, is concerned with love, compassion and care. It's about tenderness and comfort, and extending these to ourselves as well as others.

✳

Each chakra is associated with a particular colour and element, and each one focuses on a different aspect of our wellbeing.

✳

> **Chakras can be understood as a system for understanding and looking after your physical, emotional, intellectual and spiritual needs.**

THE THROAT CHAKRA, *VISHUDDHA*

Turquoise/light blue in colour, located in the throat, and related to the spirit/ether element.

The Throat Chakra is concerned with communication, self-expression and truth. It's about sharing our thoughts and feelings with others, whether that's through speech, writing, art or another form of self-expression. It's also about receiving communication – listening to and appreciating the words and thoughts of others.

THE THIRD EYE CHAKRA, *AJNA*

It's indigo/purple in colour, located at the brow, between the eyes and related to the spirit/cosmic energy element.

The Third Eye or Brow Chakra is concerned with perception, intuition and wider understanding.

It's about clarity, wisdom, imagination and ideas.

THE CROWN CHAKRA, SAHASRARA

This can be violet, white or gold in colour, at the very top of the head and related to the spirit/cosmic energy element.

The Crown Chakra is concerned with pure consciousness and connection on a higher level. It's about spirituality, inspiration and the sublime.

ELEMENTS

You'll notice that the first four chakras have elements with which we are all familiar – earth, water, fire and air – while the final three are associated with something much more ambiguous: spirit, whether ether or cosmic energy. This can be hard to grasp, as can the energy and focus of the higher chakras. The lower chakras are more practical and material, while the higher chakras are somewhat intangible and nebulous. As we explore the chakras in more detail, this will come into sharper focus.

MASLOW'S HIERARCHY OF NEEDS

You may have heard of Maslow's Hierarchy of Needs, an idea proposed by American psychologist Abraham Maslow in the 1940s. This is most often symbolized as a triangle or pyramid with different layers, from the bottom up:

• physiological needs (food, shelter and warmth)

• safety needs (security and safety)

• love and belonging needs (close relationships and friendships)

• esteem needs (feelings of accomplishment and pride in achievements)

- cognitive needs (the desire to learn and understand)

- aesthetic (the longing for beauty)

- self-actualization (realizing your potential)

- transcendence (spirituality)

Although these don't correlate exactly with the chakras, there are some interesting parallels, and it can be useful to bear this in mind, as it highlights the psychological significance of paying attention to your different levels of need and experience, even if chakras aren't really your thing.

IMAGINE A BUILDING

The Base Chakra is the foundations of the building. They have been built deep into the earth to provide a stable base. They aren't visible, and they may not get as much attention as the higher levels, but they are essential. Without them, everything else would crumble.

The Sacral Chakra is the reception area. There's a friendly reception team behind a desk, beautiful flowers in vases, comfortable seats, a map of the other floors and even a coffee shop with delicious smells. There aren't any windows, but there's a beautiful light fixture that fills the space with a warm glow.

The Solar Plexus is the morning meeting room on the first floor. It's where we interact with our colleagues and begin to make plans, and get a feel for how the day will go. There are windows, but there's not much of a view yet, and we're looking more at the things inside the office.

The Heart Chakra is the staffroom. It's where we build our relationships and learn to care for ourselves and each other. We may come here to console a colleague who is upset after a difficult morning, or to bond with our workmates over a cup of tea.

The Throat Chakra is the board room, where the most important meetings and presentations are held. This is where we learn to speak up, express ourselves and listen to others.

The Third Eye Chakra is the building's library. It has large floor-to-ceiling windows giving us impressive views of the outside world. We come here to research and learn, but also to think and reflect.

The Crown Chakra is the roof terrace. It's the very top of the building, and offers stunning 360-degree views of the world around us. We come here at the end of the day or in quiet moments to reflect on all that has happened and take some time to just be.

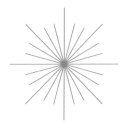

Each chakra has a symbol known as a *yantra*: these are often some variation on the lotus flower.

AGE CYCLES AND CHAKRAS

Just as each chakra is connected to a particular element and a set of characteristics, they are also linked with specific times of our lives in seven-year age cycles.

BASE CHAKRA:
Ages 0–7 and 50–56

As the Base Chakra is linked to our most essential needs, it's also connected to the earliest part of our lives, where we are in need of physical and emotional nurturing and our focus tends to be inwards. As the seven-year cycles continue, this chakra also plays a role in mid-life, when many people are reaching a stage where they might want to slow down, re-evaluate and revisit their basic needs.

THE SACRAL CHAKRA:
Ages 8–14 and 57–63

With its links to sensual pleasure, the Sacral Chakra is tied to early adolescence and our development beyond the basic survival of early years and the beginning of looking outwards, seeking play and joy and fun. This is also a time when we begin to get a sense of boundaries and our own desires. When the cycle returns to the Sacral Chakra in our late 50s and early 60s, it's a time to reconnect with pleasure and seek out the things that bring us delight.

THE SOLAR PLEXUS CHAKRA:
Ages 15–21 and 64–70

As we continue through adolescence and approach early adulthood, there is a sense of coming into our own. We have more freedom and agency, and we begin to understand our place in the world and the power we have. It's a time when our personalities develop and evolve, and when we start to explore options and possibilities for the future. When the cycle returns to this chakra in later life, it may be that we are growing into our new roles as community elders, ready to share wisdom and offer practical guidance to others. We may also feel that we are shaking off the shackles of the working world and getting ready to enjoy the freedom of retirement.

THE HEART CHAKRA: Ages 22–28 and 71–77

As we navigate early adulthood, our interpersonal relationships deepen and become increasingly meaningful. We may fall in (and out) of love, develop powerful friendships and begin to understand our parents with more compassion and knowledge as our awareness of the complexities of adulthood grows. This is also a time for healing and learning to receive love as well as giving it.

✳

As we navigate early adulthood, our interpersonal relationships deepen and become increasingly meaningful.

✳

When the cycle returns to this chakra in later life, it may come at a time when we are enjoying watching our families grow as grandchildren arrive, or it may be that we are in a place where we feel able to further extend our generosity and compassion to others, thanks to the life experiences we've had.

THE THROAT CHAKRA: Ages 29–35 and 78–84

As we fully enter adulthood and reach the age when we have increasing responsibilities, the Throat Chakra comes into its own. It's important to have a voice and express ourselves to ensure others understand our needs and desires, and it's just as important to hear those of the people around us. Communication and self-expression become increasingly valuable as we make our way through the worlds of work, potential parenthood and making a home, all while trying to maintain our own sense of self. When we return to this chakra in our late 70s and early 80s, it may be a time when we need to speak up for ourselves and ensure our needs are met as we progress into a different phase of life.

THE THIRD EYE CHAKRA: Ages 36–42 and 85–91

As we approach middle adulthood, the Third Eye Chakra is about life lessons, experience and building wisdom. As we mature, we might become less reactive and more thoughtful, and the experiences we've had will help us become more intuitive and confident in our abilities and perception. The same is true as we return to this cycle in later life; it's a time when others may come to us to seek guidance and ask us to share our wisdom.

THE CROWN CHAKRA: Ages 43–49 and 92–98

The idea of a mid-life crisis might seem quite clichéd, but it happens to many of us. By connecting with and channelling our Crown Chakra, we can try to do the inner work needed to better understand ourselves and identify where and why we might be feeling dissatisfied. It's a time for contemplation, awareness and understanding, and it's also a time when we may begin to get a greater sense of our own place within the universe. If we reach the age where the Crown Chakra returns for another life cycle, it's a time for quiet and calm, an awareness of all that has been and a sense of unity and peace.

ENERGY
FLOW

If your chakras are all well-balanced and allow energy to flow as it should, then things in your life will feel aligned, peaceful and manageable. The energy should be flowing freely through your physical and energetic body, flowing up and down the chakras.

Because energy needs to flow in both directions, no one chakra is more important than the other, even though some of the lower chakras might seem a bit more basic than the very spiritual higher ones. Each of them contributes to your overall wellbeing, and you want them all to work in harmony.

As we'll see, if there is a blockage or weakness preventing energy moving from the lower chakras to the higher, you might find that you are succeeding in certain areas of your life but have a sense of dis-ease and dissatisfaction, as if you're missing out on something more meaningful. If there is a blockage or weakness preventing

energy moving from the higher chakras to the lower, you might find that you have trouble turning an idea into reality: inspiration might not be a problem, but taking concrete steps to implement your idea becomes really challenging.

Think back to the building analogy on page 16. In order to have a successful day in the building, you need to be able to move up and down between the floors. Your time in the library (the Third Eye Chakra) won't be well-spent unless you have the skills of communication honed in the board room (the Throat Chakra); nor will you communicate effectively in the board room if you haven't built relationships with your colleagues in the staffroom (the Heart Chakra). Likewise, you need the time in the library to research and finesse your ideas so you can share them in the board room, and you might use your time reflecting on the roof terrace (the Crown Chakra) to better inform the relationships you nurture in the staffroom. Without the reception desk (the Sacral Chakra) you'd never have been able to find your

Energy needs to flow in both directions, no one chakra is more important than the other.

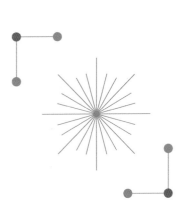

When energy is able to flow in a free...manner between all the chakras, things will feel satisfying, efficient and effective.

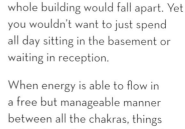

way around – and without the foundations (the Base Chakra), the whole building would fall apart. Yet you wouldn't want to just spend all day sitting in the basement or waiting in reception.

When energy is able to flow in a free but manageable manner between all the chakras, things will feel satisfying, efficient and effective. You will feel like you're getting the most out of life without over-extending yourself. You will be able to move through all the floors of the building as you need to, in order to reach your potential and have a meaningful and satisfying day.

IDENTIFYING ISSUES

Because each chakra is linked to a physical part of the body, you can use this to search for clues about potential issues. If you have a sense that something is 'off' or not working for you, but you're not sure what it is, pay attention to any physical health problems you may have been experiencing. For example, a sore throat can be a sign of issues with the Throat Chakra. Is there a situation in which you are under- (or over-) expressing yourself? Could it be that this is preventing you from progressing? Perhaps your failure to vocalize your feelings means you aren't able to move forward with a project you care about, or maybe it's stopping you from sharing something important with your partner.

Here are some common physical symptoms that can be linked to issues with each chakra.

THE BASE CHAKRA

Because of its connections to the most basic of our physical needs, issues around eating (such as under or overeating) can be linked to the Base Chakra. It can also be linked to problems with the feet, ankles and legs.

THE SACRAL CHAKRA

The Sacral Chakra can be linked to issues with sexual or reproductive health, as well as premenstrual problems. It can also be linked to pain or stiffness in the hips.

THE SOLAR PLEXUS CHAKRA

This chakra sits right over our digestive system, so it's no surprise that it can be linked to problems in this area. This is also a part of the body where we tend to hold and feel stress, so bear this in mind as well.

THE HEART CHAKRA

The Heart Chakra can be linked to issues with the heart and circulation system.

THE THROAT CHAKRA

As the name suggests, throat issues, such as a sore throat or a lost voice, can be tied to the Throat Chakra. You might also experience the feeling of a lump in your throat or vomiting. As the ears and nose are closely linked to the throat, any problems in these areas could be linked back to this chakra.

THE THIRD EYE CHAKRA

Headaches and issues with the eyes can be linked to this chakra, as can stress and anxiety that you feel very much in your head rather than in your gut.

THE CROWN CHAKRA

Again, problems with this chakra can be linked to headaches and also to high blood pressure.

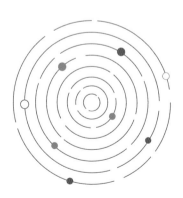

ABOUT THIS BOOK

Now that we've looked at an overview of the chakras, we're going to explore each one in more detail, starting with the Base Chakra and working our way up the spine to the Crown. For each chakra, we'll talk about the areas of our lives they can be linked to, and the sort of feelings and experiences you might have if a chakra is balanced and flowing freely, weak or blocked, or overactive (think back to the water wheel analogy on page 10). We'll also look at some different activities and exercises you can try to strengthen or unblock each chakra, and there will be journal prompts along the way so you can explore the feelings that come up for you.

At the end of the book, there is a full body-scan meditation designed to help you connect with the chakras and promote energy flow.

✳

Each chakra contributes to your overall wellbeing, and you want them all to work in harmony.

✳

THE BASE
CHAKRA

Sanskrit: *Muladhara,* meaning 'root support' or 'base support'

Colour: Red

Element: Earth

Symbol: Four-petalled lotus

Key words: Grounded, connection, earth, stability

The Base or Root Chakra is all about our connection to the earth and the physical or material world. It's about the most essential physical aspects of our being. Our most basic needs are food, shelter and warmth: without these, we can't function in other areas of our lives.

In the building analogy on page 16, we talked about the Base Chakra as being the building's foundations, embedded in the earth and creating a secure and stable base. This is needed before the architect can start thinking about beautiful sweeping staircases or stunning foyers, and before the interior designers can begin working on colour schemes and light fittings. It's also helpful to think about the roots of a tree (after all, another name for the Base Chakra is the Root Chakra). The tree's roots might not be visible, but they reach deep into the earth and draw sustenance from it, as well as ensuring the tree is stable and upright. The roots need to extend and be healthy before the tree can grow or begin to develop leaves, fruits and beautiful blossoms.

Although the Base Chakra is largely concerned with the material word, our needs for nourishment and shelter aren't just physical: we also need emotional nourishment and shelter in the form of a supportive tribe, whether our parents, family or friends.

If your Base Chakra is healthy and balanced, you will feel grounded and safe. You will feel comfortable in your situation and have a sense of security and stability. You will know where your next meal is coming from, and that you have somewhere safe to sleep. You will know who to turn to if you need support. You will feel able to manage the basic necessities of your life, including eating healthily, dealing with finances and keeping your living space in a good state. You will have a strong sense of your roots: of where you came from and how it has shaped you.

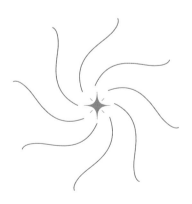

HOW CAN YOU TELL IF YOUR BASE CHAKRA IS DAMAGED OR WEAKENED?

If there are issues with your Base Chakra, you might feel a bit lost or cut adrift, as if you are somehow disconnected from the earth and the real world. You might lose interest in looking after your physical needs.

This can show up in lots of different ways: you might eat too much or not enough, you might not get the rest you need, or you might over consume in other ways, for example by drinking too much alcohol or regularly spending beyond your means.

When you lack of control and connection to the basics, parts of your life seem quite chaotic. You might let your living space become messy or dirty, and you might often make mistakes or lose things at work because you're disorganized.

You might have trouble making things happen – perhaps you have good ideas, but lack the practical ability to make them reality. Your friends might say you're a bit of a daydreamer or lost in your own head a lot.

You might have a sense of being a bit weak or unstable, as if someone is playing a game of Jenga and the tower is precariously close to toppling due to some wobbly bricks at the bottom.

If you have a damaged Base Chakra, you might find that you have real difficulty dealing with big life changes, like moving to a new place or a relationship ending, because you don't have a firm foundation to fall back on.

Lastly, it's worth remembering that sometimes, issues with the Base Chakra can be traced back to childhood. If you had an unstable childhood where your home environment and/or caregivers were inconsistent and

An overactive chakra might be spinning too fast, flooding you with too much of a certain kind of energy.

unpredictable, you may not have had the chance to put together these essential foundations. Through focused work and a great deal of self-compassion (and with support from people you trust), it is possible to strengthen your Base Chakra to give you the kind of roots or foundations you have always deserved, but if you have past trauma, you may well need some professional support in order to achieve this. If you think this is the case for you, please seek out help so you can find security and stability in the life you have now.

HOW CAN YOU TELL IF YOUR BASE CHAKRA IS OVERACTIVE?

Just as it's possible for a chakra to be weak or damaged, it can also be overactive. If you consider the idea of the chakras as spinning wheels of light, an overactive chakra might be spinning too fast, flooding you with too much of a certain kind of energy or keeping that energy in one place so that you become trapped.

To use the building analogy once more, the foundations are essential in order to provide the building with a stable and secure base, but they also need to be designed in a way that has a certain amount of flexibility in order to allow the building to absorb the shock of things like storms or earthquakes. If the building's foundations are too rigid, everything can shatter.

If your Base Chakra is too active, you might be very stubborn, prone to digging your heels in and strongly resistant to change. You might feel quite heavy, as if your legs are leaden and your whole being is weighed down. You may want to stay in the same job for years, even though you're stagnating, or you might refuse to alter your regular daily routine even though something really important has come up. You might be deeply resistant to travel or trying new things. There's nothing wrong with ordering your favourite dish at a restaurant, but you could be missing out on so many other flavours and experiences if you refuse to consider even trying anything else.

People may find you a bit predictable or boring, or say that you hold on to old ideas and beliefs without considering other points of view.

Essentially, you may be stuck in a rut, somewhat curmudgeonly before your time, and so set in your ways that you're missing much of the beauty of life.

HOW TO CARE FOR YOUR BASE CHAKRA

A healthy chakra is either balanced or active, with a healthy flow of energy in and out, functioning as intended. If this isn't the case, there are things you can try to help strengthen or balance your Base Chakra.

GET OUT INTO NATURE

Due to this chakra's strong links with the earth, surrounding yourself with nature is a great way to feel more connected with it. If you have access to the countryside, try taking a walk in nature, whether that's in woodland, on a moor, through fields or along the coast. Allow yourself to move slowly and notice the natural world around you – the leaves on the trees, the earth on the ground, the animals and insects you come across.

If you have a garden, you could go and sit outside in this green space and spend some time being at one with it. Try sitting on the ground or walking barefoot in order to create a sense of connection between you and the earth. Imagine the energy from the earth flowing up through your feet and legs and along your spine. In the same way, imagine the unwanted energy in your body flowing out and into the earth. If you can, thrust your hands into the soil and smell the earth.

If you live in a more urban area and don't have the option of sitting in a garden or going on a countryside stroll, seek out whatever small green pockets you can. Look for a city park or a flower bed. Even in built-up areas, you will often find trees or even small weeds pushing their way up through the concrete. Notice whatever examples of nature you can and allow yourself to focus on them and their links with the earth and our most essential nature.

ORGANIZE YOUR LIVING SPACE

If you feel like you are somewhat adrift and chaotic in your life, try spending some time getting organized in your living space. There's a lot about the world we can't control, but we can try and create a sense of order and harmony within the small spaces we call our own. Spend some time deliberately and mindfully organizing your home. Try to make it somewhere you can see as a sanctuary. Put things away in their proper places and try to make sure it feels like a safe place to be.

Through focused work and a great deal of self-compassion... it is possible to strengthen your Base Chakra

Putting together a routine can help you feel a sense of order and control as you move through your day.

GET YOUR FINANCES IN ORDER

Money worries can make us feel completely out of control and anxious, and yet so often they are self-perpetuating; if we are low on cash, we may be more likely to overspend, even on things we don't need, because we're scrabbling around trying to feel a sense of control and satisfaction. A person with a well-balanced Base Chakra will usually have a good grip on their finances. This doesn't necessarily mean they have lots of money, but can instead mean they know how much money they do have, they've worked out a budget so they know how much they can spend, and they tend not to rely on spending

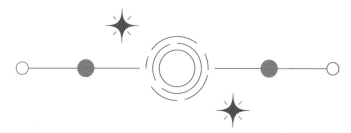

as a way to make themselves feel better. Spending some time educating yourself about finances and budgeting and working on your relationship with money can really help with achieving the kind of stability that comes with a balanced Base Chakra.

BUILD A ROUTINE

In a similar vein to the points above, putting together a basic routine can help you to feel a little more stable and grounded in your day-to-day life. Perhaps you didn't have the kind of childhood where you knew what would be happening from one day to the next – gift yourself that knowledge and stability now. Try

to incorporate some of the other practices suggested here into your routine, such as exercise and eating well. Putting together a routine can help you feel a sense of order and control as you move through your day – just remember to allow for some flexibility and change as well.

REACH OUT FOR RED

Red is the colour associated with the Base Chakra, so if you want to work on this chakra, try bringing the colour into your life as a positive reminder of where to focus your attention. You might buy red flowers to brighten up your living space, or wear something red, like a red top, lipstick or nail polish. Eating red foods can be a great way to connect too: try apples, red berries, cherries or even a glass of red wine. Pay attention to the colour in the world around you and use each time you see it as an opportunity to mindfully ground yourself and feel the energy of the earth rising through your feet.

CONNECT WITH LOVED ONES

One of the best ways to feel a sense of safety and security is to surround ourselves with people whom we love and trust. Try spending time with family or friends who make you feel comfortable and at ease. Enjoy the stability and sense of support that comes from being around people who care for you. Extend that sense of nurture and care to them as well. When we feel disconnected or cut off, it can be easy to shut ourselves away, but spending some time basking in the warmth and comfort of your tribe can work wonders.

EXERCISE

Exercise can help us feel more present in our own bodies and therefore more connected to the physical and material world. If you feel like you're getting wrapped up in your mind, perhaps consumed with worries or drifting off into distracting daydreams, use exercise as a way to connect with and occupy your physical body. Slow, measured movements like those found in yoga and Pilates can be particularly useful here, but you might also relish the chance to go for a run, feeling your feet connect with the earth with each step. This is a chance to be present in your body, so don't listen to music or podcasts as you work out. Just feel the movement and revel in it.

EAT HEALTHY, WHOLESOME FOODS

As we've seen, the Base Chakra is about essential physical needs and survival, so it makes sense that eating can help you to connect with and strengthen this chakra. Focus on eating wholesome, healthy foods that will fuel and nourish your body. Eating plant-based foods, especially root vegetables, can be a particularly effective way of feeling more grounded and connected with the earth. Try to take the time to eat your meals mindfully, appreciating each bite and thinking about how the food is supporting your body.

Pay attention to the colour in the world around you ...feel the energy of the earth rising through your feet.

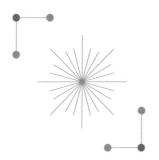

IF YOUR BASE CHAKRA IS OVERACTIVE

If your Base Chakra is overactive, you might want to try some of the exercises for strengthening the higher chakras, as these can also help to balance and calm your Base Chakra. See 'How to care for your Third Eye Chakra' on page 104 and 'How to care for your Crown Chakra' on page 114.

You could also try having a decluttering session and getting rid of any items that you no longer need or which feel somehow heavy to you. Sometimes we hold on to things that carry difficult memories or associations, and they can weigh us down and hold us in place. Letting go can help you feel lighter and less stuck. In the same way, if you are so set in a particular routine that it's starting to interfere with your happiness, challenge yourself to make one small change each day (or each week) to help you begin to loosen your rigid boundaries and allow a little more space in your life for spontaneity.

MEDITATION: ROOTS

Find a calm, quiet place where you won't be disturbed for about 10 or 15 minutes. Read this meditation through before you begin, so that you can close your eyes and focus on it.

1. Sit in a chair with your back straight and your feet firmly planted on the ground. If you prefer, you can sit cross-legged on the floor, perhaps with one hand touching the ground. The important thing is to be in contact with the floor.

2. Take a few deep breaths, breathing slowly and mindfully. Pay attention to the way the ground feels beneath you. With each inhale, allow yourself to imagine the energy of the earth flowing through your feet; with each exhale, imagine unwanted energy leaving your body and dissipating into the earth.

3. In your mind's eye, picture a tree. Imagine the branches, the leaves. Think about the texture of the bark and the solidity of the trunk. Now allow your gaze to move down the tree, from the very tops of the branches, down the trunk, to the earth. Imagine you can see through the earth;

picture the network of roots reaching deeply into the soil, holding the tree firmly in place and drawing nourishment.

4. Spend some time with this mental image, allowing yourself to consider the sense of stability, longevity and groundedness that it creates.

5. When you're ready, take a few more deep breaths and open your eyes. Try to hold the energy of the tree with you as you move through your day.

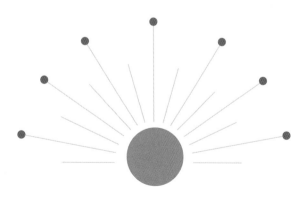

JOURNAL PROMPT: A SAFE PLACE

✳

Think about a space that makes you feel safe and calm. It could be a space from your childhood – perhaps your first bedroom, or the kitchen at your grandparents' house. If this isn't an option for you, choose a space from another time in your life, or from right now. It could even be somewhere you haven't physically been: a place from a favourite book or film where you feel sure you would feel comfortable and secure. Write about the space, describing it in as much detail as you can. As you write, imagine that you are there, in the space, and write about how it feels to be there. What is it about the space that makes it feel so grounding and safe? Is there anything about it that you can recreate in your day-to-day life, to return to when things get overwhelming?

THE SACRAL CHAKRA

Sanskrit: *Svadhisthana*, meaning 'where your being is' or 'where your being is established'

Colour: Orange

Element: Water

Symbol: Six-petalled lotus

Key words: Feelings, sensuality, movement

The Sacral Chakra is all about being in your body and the sheer dizzying wonderfulness of being alive, and all the feelings and sensations that go along with it. While the Base Chakra is about the bare essentials needed for survival, the Sacral Chakra is about physical joy and delight. This chakra is connected with sensual pleasures, from eating delicious food to inhaling intoxicating aromas or enjoying sexual exploration.

This is a very playful chakra, as when it's balanced and in harmony it enables us to explore and create and enjoy; essentially, it's about playing, without self-consciousness or worry.

The Sacral Chakra is found in part of the body that is geared towards pleasure and creativity. When your Sacral Chakra is working as it should be, the energy that flows through it will mean you are at ease in your body, full of optimism and joy. You will enjoy being physical, taking pleasure in things like movement, dancing, exercise and sex. You will feel energetic and engaged, interested in your surroundings and connected to the people around you. You will have a sense of open-mindedness and feel safe being vulnerable and open with others (as well as helping them feel safe and at ease around you). You will be playful and open to spontaneity, but still have a healthy sense of your own personal boundaries.

You will get pleasure from interacting with other people and building relationships, whether these are romantic or platonic, and you will have a sense of being able to go with the flow and enjoy life as it comes.

HOW CAN YOU TELL IF YOUR SACRAL CHAKRA IS DAMAGED OR WEAKENED?

If your Sacral Chakra is weak or damaged, you might feel joyless or even depressed. You might not feel anything at all, instead being numb, disinterested and disconnected from life, and perhaps even from things that have previously been a real source of enjoyment.

You might be quite insular, avoiding social occasions and behaving in quite a cold or awkward manner when you do interact with others. You may feel uncomfortable at social events or feel like you're somehow missing the mark and not connecting with the people around you. You might wonder why everyone else seems able to be so relaxed and at ease with each other when you feel stiff and cold. If a friend or loved one experiences a success, you might feel jealous or bitter instead of being proud of and delighted for them.

Due to the Sacral Chakra's strong links with physical sensations and pleasure, it's no surprise to hear that a weak Sacral Chakra can have a real impact on your sex drive. You may feel little to no interest in sex, or find ways to avoid it altogether.

This lack of interest in the sensual can extend to a general sense of discomfort in the physical body. You might feel awkward or uncomfortable in your own skin. Perhaps you avoid dancing because you think you will look foolish or clumsy; maybe

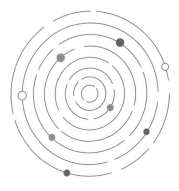

The Sacral Chakra is all about being in your body and the sheer dizzying wonderfulness of being alive.

you don't want to go to the swimming pool or the beach because you hate how your body looks without clothes on. You might avoid exercise and have a sense of your whole body being sluggish and stagnant.

People with a weakened or damaged Sacral Chakra often bury themselves in work, and may feel under a great deal of stress due to stretching themselves too thin and taking on too many serious commitments. You may have a sense that you don't have time to

This is a very playful chakra when it's balanced and in harmony.

do fun things – or perhaps that you don't deserve to do them.

You might find it hard to be silly or playful, and find that you feel very self-conscious in situations that might require you to be vulnerable or light-hearted. Friends may mutter that you take yourself too seriously. You may have a sense of being rigid and stiff, with no idea of how to break this pattern.

HOW CAN YOU TELL IF YOUR SACRAL CHAKRA IS OVERACTIVE?

If your Sacral Chakra is overactive, this can play out in overindulgent or even addictive behaviours. You may be over-spontaneous, acting without taking the time to consider potential consequences. You might move rapidly from one sensual experience to another, whether that's over-eating, drinking too much, or taking part in frequent and potentially risky sexual behaviour. You may find that you seek out very casual sexual encounters in an effort to feel something physical without getting the deep sensual connection that comes from making love to someone with whom you feel truly engaged and involved.

An overactive Sacral Chakra can leave you feeling overstimulated and overwhelmed, as if you're feeling too much. You may find you're unable to settle or commit to anything because you're always seeking out the next new experience. You may behave in quite a selfish way, prioritizing your own pleasure over the needs of others. You may feel as if you're living life 'on the surface', moving from one experience or encounter to another without really feeling anything on a more meaningful emotional, intellectual or spiritual level.

HOW TO CARE FOR YOUR SACRAL CHAKRA

A healthy Sacral Chakra allows you to enjoy many of the most profound and special experiences of being human. Finding ways to care for and balance this sensual, delightful chakra can bring great joy into your life.

GO TO THE WATER

The Sacral Chakra is associated with the element of water, so finding a way to be around water can be a brilliant way of caring for it. Perhaps you could go swimming, enjoying the exhilarating feeling of the cool water rushing over your skin and the wonderful stretch in your limbs as you move through the sea or pool. You may decide to pay homage to the water element and your Sacral Chakra with a sensual bath: run a warm bath, fill it with bubbles or oils (try sandalwood, jasmine or ylang-ylang), and lie in luxurious comfort (you may even decide to invite your lover to join you). Another great option can be to get out on the water in a boat,

whether that's a sailing boat or a canoe. Enjoy the sound of the waves lapping against your vessel and take the time to enjoy the freedom and flow of the water.

GET A MASSAGE

Getting a massage can be a wonderful way to connect with your body on a sensual level. You might ask your partner to give you a massage, or you may prefer to go to a professional massage therapist. Try to focus on the feeling of the massage as it eases pressure in your body and relaxes your muscles. Remember that you deserve this experience.

EAT FOR PLEASURE

Without drifting into excessive overindulgence, taking the time to eat a special meal or a particularly delicious treat can help you connect with your Sacral Chakra and take delight in physical pleasures. Try a bowl of your favourite ice cream with a velvety chocolate sauce, or a bowlful of fruit packed with colour and flavour.

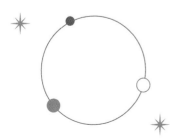

There is no better way to connect with the physical pleasure of being in the body than to move it.

A healthy Sacral Chakra can help us enjoy fulfilling and satisfying sex.

MOVE YOUR BODY

There is no better way to connect with the physical pleasure of being in the body than to move it. With a focus on sensuality and joy, try putting on your favourite song and dancing. Let go of inhibitions and just let the music flow through you, delighting in your body as you move.

PLAY

As adults, we so rarely allow ourselves time to play. If you have children in your life, sit down with them and play together. If you don't, you can still play – and it's a wonderful, joyful thing to do. Try a form of play where you can really feel things: you might decide to jump on a trampoline or sit on a swing, or you may choose to sit down with some paints and get messy. Try using your fingers, and don't get hung up on what the final product looks like. Just play around and enjoy it.

BE INTIMATE

A healthy Sacral Chakra can help us enjoy fulfilling and satisfying sex. If you're not in a place where you feel interested in sex, you could try being intimate with your partner in other ways, whether through massage (see above) or enjoying some kissing or light touching without any pressure for things to go further until you both feel like it.

MAKE TODAY SPECIAL

Many of us have the tendency to save things for 'a special occasion'. Do you have a stash of unopened gourmet treats, unused toiletries, unworn clothes and unused bedding or towels because you are saving them 'for a special occasion'? Make today a special occasion: light the candle, wear your favourite outfit, make a delicious meal and eat it with all your nicest tableware. Why not have a candlelit three-course meal on a Tuesday? Why not wear a silky-smooth dress on a Saturday morning? Allow yourself to enjoy sensual pleasures and indulgences that you may have subconsciously been denying yourself.

INDULGE IN ORANGE

The Sacral Chakra is associated with all things orange, and what could be more appropriate? This vibrant, energizing colour is bursting with joy. Find ways to bring a splash of orange into your life, whether you enjoy a deliciously juicy tangerine, accessorize your outfit with a bright orange scarf or use an orange highlighter to bring a zing of colour to your workday. Look for orange foods and flowers, or head outside at sunset to see the sky painted with a range of golden tones.

START A CREATIVE PROJECT

With the Sacral Chakra's links to giving birth to new creations, you could try to activate it by beginning a new creative project. Of course, if your Sacral Chakra is weak or damaged, being creative can be challenging, but setting the intention and trying to get started can help to awaken the chakra and get things spinning. Remember to be patient with yourself and seek to enjoy the process.

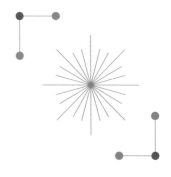

IF YOUR SACRAL CHAKRA IS OVERACTIVE

If you have an overactive Sacral Chakra, some of the activities for balancing higher chakras may be useful – see 'How to care for your Third Eye Chakra' on page 50 and 'How to care for your Crown Chakra' on page 114.

While mindfulness meditation techniques can be a great way to help you connect more strongly with your Sacral Chakra by noticing and enjoying things moment by moment, they can also help you to slow down and take a more deliberate approach to things like eating, drinking, sex and decision-making. Taking the time to eat slowly and mindfully, for example (see next exercise), means you still get to notice and enjoy all the pleasure of a delicious food, without falling into overconsumption or addictive behaviours.

MEDITATION: MINDFUL EATING

As explained previously, a mindful eating meditation can be useful for balancing and connecting with your Sacral Chakra whether it's over- or underactive. The sense most closely associated with the Sacral Chakra is taste, making this meditation ideal in more ways than one. Read the text below through in full before you begin so you can focus completely on the experience.

1. Choose something small to eat. It could be a square of chocolate, a grape, or perhaps a slice of a juicy, ripe fruit like a nectarine or a segment of orange.

2. Sit in a calm, quiet place where you won't be disturbed for a few minutes. Look at the piece of food: examine the colour, and consider the texture and the weight of it. Lift it to your nose and smell it, allowing the aroma to fill your nostrils.

3. Now place the piece of food in your mouth. Hold it on your tongue for a moment or so. Allow the flavours to begin to register, and notice them: is it sweet, sharp, salty, sour? What does the food feel like on your tongue? If it's a piece of chocolate, it may start to melt a little. If it's fruit, you may notice the juiciness. When you're ready, you can slowly begin to chew, releasing still more flavour. Take the time to eat the food slowly and mindfully, trying to notice every part of the experience.

4. When you're done, your mouth will feel alive with the sensations. Try to carry that sense of energy and delight with you throughout the day.

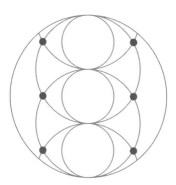

JOURNAL PROMPT: FREE WRITING

Because the Sacral Chakra is linked with spontaneity and playfulness, experiment with some free writing in your journal. Set a timer for 10 or 15 minutes, sit somewhere quiet and wait for the words to flow. If nothing comes, you can just start moving the pen over the paper, scribbling or sketching, and see if that helps. Don't worry about whether it makes sense or what it means; just let the words come. Give your body and mind the freedom to explore the page and create. If that means that you just fill the page with squiggles and lines, that's fine. Enjoy creating the squiggles and lines. Feel the way the pen moves across the page, notice the colour of the ink and the texture of the paper. Experience the moment without trying to control or influence it. You may find that, once you give things the chance to flow, you have rather a lot to say.

THE SOLAR PLEXUS CHAKRA

Sanskrit: *Manipura*, meaning 'place of gems' or 'place of jewels'

Colour: Yellow

Element: Fire

Symbol: Ten-petalled lotus

Key words: Power, vitality, motivation

The Solar Plexus Chakra is all about personal power. It's a bold chakra that can fizz and buzz with energy and fill you with a sense of confidence in your own abilities. So many of us are prone to bouts of self-doubt and imposter syndrome, so this is a really important chakra when it comes to navigating the workplace as well as your personal life.

When your Solar Plexus Chakra is balanced and functioning optimally, you will feel calm, confident and in control. You will have a sense of being in your own lane and moving forward with a steady and sustainable focus. You will be motivated and driven, able to be productive and consistent. You will have a clear awareness of your goals and what you need to do to achieve them, and you will feel able to work diligently and carefully to make things happen. You will engage with hard work and effort with relish, but you will also have a clear idea of what your boundaries are, and your self-worth will be strong enough for you to step away and take breaks when they're needed. Your focus and ability to plan will make you a natural leader, and others will seek you out for advice on getting things done.

The Solar Plexus Chakra is also linked to that sense of intuition that we feel in this part of the body: what we usually call 'a gut feeling'. If your Solar Plexus Chakra is healthy and functioning well, you'll feel confident in seeing your plans through.

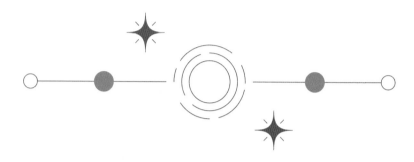

HOW CAN YOU TELL IF YOUR SOLAR PLEXUS CHAKRA IS DAMAGED OR WEAKENED?

If your Solar Plexus Chakra is weak or damaged in some way, you might be prone to feelings of overwhelm or have a general sense of directionlessness in life. You might feel quite weak or easily led, and it may be that others see you as something of a pushover. The ability to compromise is a valuable thing, but it should be a two-way street. If you feel like you're always going along with what others want rather than what you want, whether around something relatively minor like which restaurant to go to or what to watch on TV, or something more significant, like a big financial decision or life move, then it's possible your Solar Plexus Chakra needs some help.

You might be quite a nervous person who suffers from anxiety and low self-esteem. You may also find decision-making really difficult, agonizing over which choice to go with and doubting yourself even after you've made a call.

You may be lacking in focus or drive to the extent that your life is full of half-finished projects, from a partly painted room to a pair of unused running shoes.

You may also have a fear of failure. Nobody actively enjoys failing, but if you're so worried about getting things wrong that you don't even try, you are holding yourself back. You may be so reluctant to put yourself out there that you stay firmly in your box. This is very different to staying 'in your lane', because you're not moving forward.

✳
The Solar Plexus Chakra is...a bold chakra that can fizz and buzz with energy and fill you with a sense of confidence.
✳

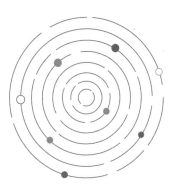

If your Solar Plexus Chakra is overactive, you may find that you're no longer driven by your goals.

HOW CAN YOU TELL IF YOUR SOLAR PLEXUS CHAKRA IS OVERACTIVE?

Most of us know or have known someone with an overactive Solar Plexus Chakra. When this chakra is spinning out of control, it can lead to arrogant, egotistical and even controlling behaviour.

If your Solar Plexus Chakra is overactive, you may find that you're no longer driven by your goals. Instead, they are driving you – and if you work too hard, they may be driving you straight into burnout.

You might be prone to frustration and angry outbursts when things don't go the way you want them to, and you particularly struggle with not being in control. This means that things like travel delays or issues caused by someone else's mistake can be extremely challenging for you and may provoke a disproportionate reaction.

Even if you don't allow the effects of your overactive Solar Plexus Chakra to spill out into how you treat other people, you may still hold yourself to such high standards that they can interfere with your enjoyment of life. You might have a tendency to get caught up in things that make you feel important, like organizing unnecessary meetings or failing to delegate tasks to others. This can cause you to miss the things that really matter. For example, you may miss out on a family event because there's a big deal going through at work and you're convinced it would be disastrous if you're not in the office when in happens – even if your boss has said it's fine for you to go.

HOW TO CARE FOR YOUR SOLAR PLEXUS CHAKRA

A healthy Solar Plexus Chakra can help you achieve the things you really want to in life, and imbue you with a sense of confidence and self-worth.

FIVE MINUTES OF EXERCISE

If you are getting caught up in feelings of self-doubt or uncertainty, set a timer for five minutes and complete some vigorous exercise, like star jumps, push-ups or even running up and down the stairs. This will get your blood flowing and force you back into your own body rather than your head, helping you to get perspective and feel a stronger sense of self. It will also interrupt the cycle of doubt or indecision, which can be so hard to escape from.

BREATHE THROUGH STRESS

If you're feeling overwhelmed by stress and leaping up to do a few star jumps isn't an option (perhaps because you're in the middle of a meeting and your colleagues might find it a little distracting!), then try to take a few deep breaths to breathe through the stress. Place your hand on your stomach above the navel, in the area of your Solar

Plexus Chakra. Take a deep breath into this part of your body and pay attention to the way your hand lifts up as the breath fills the space. Hold it for a moment or two, then exhale. Do this a few more times, imagining the energy and power of the Solar Plexus Chakra flowing into the rest of your body with each breath.

✳

It's a bold chakra that can fizz and buzz with energy and fill you with a sense of confidence in your own abilities.

✳

*

Breathe deeply and fully into your Solar Plexus and allow the powerful posture to bring you a sense of confidence and strength.

*

BREAK DOWN TASKS INTO SMALL GOALS AND CELEBRATE EACH WIN

As a healthy Solar Plexus Chakra enables us to work diligently towards our goals, try to channel this energy even when you don't feel driven or motivated. The most common reason for losing motivation is because a task feels too big or even impossible, and we become overwhelmed. Next time this happens, try to break the main goal down into smaller parts. Then break those down into even smaller parts. Write them all down in a list so you know what you need to do, in order. For example, if the overall goal is to research, write and give a presentation for work, break it down into parts – first research, then writing, then presenting – and break these down again, and again if you need to, until the first thing on the list feels achievable. If the first thing is 'sit at my desk and read two pages of this article',

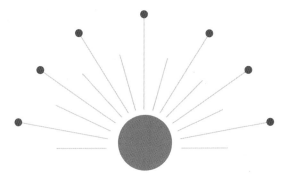

that's a lot less intimidating than the overall task. At each stage, stop and celebrate your success, and let them energize you as you move on to the next step of the task.

PAY ATTENTION TO YOUR POSTURE

Our posture and the way we present ourselves can have a huge impact on the way others see us – and on the way we see ourselves. How are you sitting or standing right now? Are you hunched over, head bowed, spine curled in an almost defensive posture? How does that look to others? And how does it feel to you? If we sit or stand in a way that suggests we're trying to hide or shield ourselves, we're going to feel weak, vulnerable and ineffective. Whenever you remember to, square your shoulders, unclench your jaw, straighten your spine and allow your face to relax into a soft, easy smile. Breathe deeply and fully into your Solar Plexus and allow the powerful posture to bring you a sense of confidence and strength.

PRACTISE SETTING BOUNDARIES

Setting boundaries can be a really good way to assert ourselves and connect with our own personal power, but it's not always easy to do. Practise by setting smaller, more manageable boundaries so that you get used to the idea of saying 'no' when you need to. This could be something like deciding not to respond to a work email after 7pm, or telling a friend who asks for too many favours that you're busy the next time they request a lift or hit you up for free babysitting. As you grow more comfortable with setting boundaries, you will be able to identify other areas of your life where more boundaries and confidence are needed.

GLOW INTO YELLOW

Bring a splash of sunshine yellow into your life to help you connect with and strengthen your Solar Plexus Chakra. Try placing a vase of daffodils or sunflowers on your desk at work to bring this bold yellow energy into your workplace, or wear a yellow hairband or tie for a rush of colour. Yellow foods such as zingy lemons and juicy pineapples will give you a boost – or eat a banana for a hit of potassium and Solar Plexus power. This chakra is associated with

the element of fire, so try lighting candles to fill your space with a fiery yellow glow.

IF YOUR SOLAR PLEXUS CHAKRA IS OVERACTIVE

If you're usually the one who plans and controls everything, try some exercises to relinquish the steering wheel and take a turn in the passenger seat. Arrange to go on a day trip with friends where you're not in charge, or let someone else lead the next project at work.

If you know you're getting caught up in overwork, make plans to leave the office by a certain time each evening – but watch out for this becoming another thing to control! Pay close attention to how you speak to others, and make a considered effort to avoid any arrogant or overpowering behaviour.

✳

Bring a splash of sunshine yellow into your life to help you connect with and strengthen your Solar Plexus Chakra.

✳

MEDITATION: A CANDLE

Find a calm, quiet place where you can sit uninterrupted for 10 or 15 minutes. Sit upright in a chair or cross-legged on a floor, with a candle on a flat surface in front of you. The candle should be at eye level if possible. When you're ready, light the candle, then take some deep breaths and sit gazing softly into the flame.

1. Look at the shape of the flame and the way it moves. Look at the colour. Listen closely to see if you can hear the sound of the wick burning or the flame flickering. Place your hand softly on your stomach over your Solar Plexus Chakra and breathe in and out, in and out, as you watch the flame. Consider the way the candle burns: it's bright and bold, but still controlled. It's not like a fire, consuming everything in its path. It's contained, held on the wick, shining brightly and giving off a golden glow.

2. Sit with the candle for 10 or 15 minutes, then when you're ready, blow it out. Try to carry that sense of self-contained power and energy with you throughout the day.

JOURNAL PROMPT: BURNING BRIGHT

Think of a time when you felt bright, confident and ambitious, with a clear idea of a goal in mind and a certainty that you knew what you needed to do to achieve it. Write about that experience. What was it like? Where in your body did you feel that sense of certainty? What was it like – empowering? Scary? A bit surreal? How did you make it happen? How did it turn out? Write about it all in as much detail as you can, trying to channel the sense of confidence you felt.

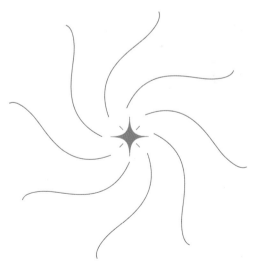

THE HEART
CHAKRA

Sanskrit: *Anahata*, meaning 'unstruck' or 'boundless'

Colour: Green

Element: Air

Symbol: Twelve-petalled lotus containing a six-pointed star or '*shatkona*'.

Key words: Compassion, unconditional love, healing

The Heart Chakra sits at the heart of the body in both senses, as it is in the very centre, halfway between the lower, more physical, chakras and the upper, more spiritual, ones.

As the name suggests, the Heart Chakra is concerned with matters of the heart. This chakra is all about unconditional love, compassion, respect and kindness. It's not just about romantic love: it's about deep, meaningful relationships with people, places and ideas of experiences. It's about a sense of benevolence, care and generosity, and true, heartfelt connection.

Balance is important here. The Heart Chakra is not just about giving love, but receiving it too. Many of us are able to extend loving feelings towards others but are less comfortable or confident receiving them, as we might worry we're somehow not worthy or deserving.

When your Heart Chakra is balanced and functioning as it should, you will be able to enjoy meaningful and fulfilling relationships with the people around you, connecting on a deep emotional level. You will be comfortable trusting the people you love and being vulnerable with them. You will enjoy emotional connections to places and memories or ideas, too, finding joy and comfort in them.

You will be emotionally intelligent and connected to your feelings, able to understand your wants and desires and accepting the wants and desires of others in a non-judgemental way. You'll understand if someone is upset or angry, and you'll be able to draw the boundaries you need to when you need them. You will refrain from manipulative behaviour and have a warm, positive and friendly approach to life.

Most of all, you will be able to extend warm, loving care to others and also to wrap it around yourself, giving yourself the time, attention and respect you need to live an emotionally balanced life.

HOW CAN YOU TELL IF YOUR HEART CHAKRA IS DAMAGED OR WEAKENED?

If your Heart Chakra is weakened or damaged, you might feel disconnected from loved ones. You may feel a somewhat hurt or bitter when you think about other people's loving relationships, and have a sense that you are somehow outside this. You may have a tendency to keep your heart closed, trying to distance yourself from others and reluctant to let anyone in.

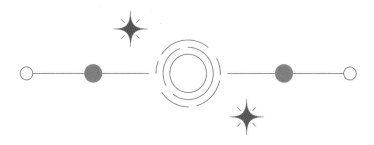

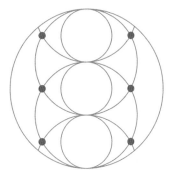

You may have low self-esteem and feel unworthy of or unable to accept love from others. This can leave you with a reluctance to be vulnerable or put yourself out there because you're afraid of being hurt or rejected. You might also hold on to resentment or feelings of hurt or betrayal rather than working through them or trying to heal. It feels safer to stay away, whether you're talking about lovers, friends or family.

If the Heart Chakra is overactive, you may be oversensitive and easily drawn into emotional drama.

A weakened Heart Chakra can leave you feeling very lonely and detached, and you may find there are moments in your life where you can't get as much enjoyment from things because you don't have anyone to share them with.

Experiences of heartbreak or bereavement can cause damage to the Heart Chakra and leave it weakened or effectively shut down. This can be devastating, but by slowly trying to open up and extend love, first to ourselves and then to others, we can heal.

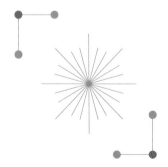

HOW CAN YOU TELL IF YOUR HEART CHAKRA IS OVERACTIVE?

If the Heart Chakra is overactive, you may be oversensitive and easily drawn into emotional drama. If you find yourself eagerly gossiping with friends about romantic disasters or trying to involve yourself in other people's relationships, it could be a sign that your Heart Chakra is spinning out of control.

Empathy is a beautiful gift, but if you're a highly sensitive person, you may become drained or overwhelmed through over-empathizing, and you may forget your own wants and needs in favour of prioritizing those of others. If this happens, it's a good sign that your Heart Chakra is overworking and you need to secure some boundaries in order to protect yourself.

In some cases, you may get so involved in the rush of feelings associated with emotional drama that you become addicted to the chaos and actively seek out emotionally charged and intense situations in order to get your fix. This isn't sustainable and can cause real damage to your own wellbeing and your relationships with others.

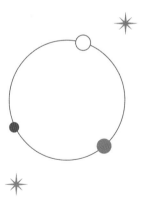

HOW TO CARE FOR YOUR HEART CHAKRA

A healthy Heart Chakra allows you to enjoy meaningful and loving connections with other people as well as taking pleasure in your own company. Finding ways to care for this beautiful chakra can bring a sense of calm and loving balance into your life.

CARE FOR A PLANT

Caring for a plant, whether that's in your garden or one in a pot, can be a simple and satisfying way to strengthen your Heart Chakra. Paying attention to the plant's needs – water, nutrition, light, pruning – is a practical reflection of the act of showing care and compassion to others. And as you invest time and care in this relationship, you will see the plant grow from strength to strength, as a powerful reminder of how love and affection help each of us grow. It's also a wonderful way to get a little green into your life.

GO FOR GREEN

We tend to associate hearts with shades of pink and red, but the key colour for the Heart Chakra is actually green. Green is a hue that suggests new beginnings and growth, nurture and abundance, and so it's the perfect colour for this generous and loving chakra. Try to find ways to bring a pop of green into your day to help remind you to connect with your Heart Chakra.

Care for a plant, wear emeralds, or eat delicious green foods. It's no coincidence that naturally green foods are deeply nourishing, so enjoy leafy greens, crisp green apples, creamy avocados and crunchy cucumbers as a way to care for yourself and your Heart Chakra. You could also seek out green spaces, like woodland or parks, and allow them to imbue you with a sense of calm and wellbeing.

TRY AEROBIC EXERCISE

With its strong links to the physical heart, a great way to revitalize the Heart Chakra is to do some aerobic exercise to get your heart pumping and flood you with positive energy. Try running, dancing, or an engaging exercise class. It's even better if you can choose something fun and do it with a friend or loved one, so you can enjoy the experience together.

✦
Green is a hue that suggests new beginnings and growth, nurture and abundance.
✦

> In Buddhism, the practice of meta or loving-kindness is a beautiful way to send a sense of compassionate wellbeing out into the world.

START A GRATITUDE PRACTICE

Practising gratitude can seem a little bit strange at first, but it can be deeply rewarding and really help you find pleasure and joy in the every day. It's about more than simply saying thank you when someone does something for you; it's about taking the time to deeply reflect on the things in your life that bring you meaning and pleasure, and to nurture a sense of appreciation for them. It can be big things, like the home you live in or the partner whom you adore, but also smaller things: you can focus on your gratitude for the cup of tea you're drinking, the plate of food in front of you, the fact that you were able to catch your bus because the driver spotted you hurrying and waited a few extra moments at the stop. Taking the time to notice and value these things, big and small, helps to open our hearts and fill us with a sense of wellbeing.

One of the simplest ways to start an effective gratitude practice is simply to sit down every evening, perhaps just before bed, and list three things you are grateful for that day. They don't have to be profound; just something that you really appreciate.

Over time, this will become an almost automatic habit, and as you move through your day, you will notice little hits of gratitude filling you with warmth and love.

MAKE A MEAL FOR SOMEONE YOU CARE ABOUT

Preparing a meal for someone is a great way to show them love and care. You are taking the time to choose something they'll enjoy, and you're offering them nourishment and enjoyment. Sitting down to share food together is one of the simplest yet most rewarding experiences we can have. It helps us feel connected and cared for,

and a lovingly prepared meal with a close friend, lover or family member feeds the soul as well as the stomach.

HAVE A HUG

The sense of touch is associated with the Heart Chakra, so take a moment today and enjoy a warm embrace with someone you care about. We humans are tactile creatures, and research has shown that a hug can release oxytocin, serotonin and dopamine, often referred to as 'feel-good hormones'.

They make us feel warm, safe and comforted – all feelings associated with the Heart Chakra. Sharing a hug with someone helps you feel connected with them, and it's also a situation in which you are being vulnerable and open with the other person, helping to build a sense of togetherness and trust.

IF YOUR HEART CHAKRA IS OVERACTIVE

If your Heart Chakra is working overtime and you are getting caught up in tangled emotional webs, it's important to take a step back and try to get some perspective and a sense of space. If you have been rushing from one romantic encounter to another without building a meaningful connection, consider taking some time to be on your own and focus on you.

Trying some of the grounding exercises in this book, like the Roots Meditation on page 41, can help you to refocus and slow down if you think you're getting carried away or caught up in emotional intensity.

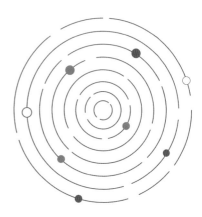

MEDITATION: LOVING-KINDNESS

In Buddhism, the practice of meta or loving-kindness is a beautiful way to send a sense of compassionate wellbeing out into the world. There are a number of traditional meta meditations you can try, but we'll begin with a simplified version here.

1. To begin with, come up with a loving mantra. It could be something like, 'May I be safe, may I be calm, may I be happy, may I be free.'

2. Sit in a calm, quiet space where you won't be interrupted. Breathe slowly and deeply, and allow yourself to settle and become still. When you're ready, think about a moment in which you have felt truly loved and cared for: perhaps a moment when a friend or loved one reached out to you when you needed support. Try to focus on that warm glow that comes with feeling loved. Now turn that glow on yourself, shining that love and compassion inwards. Aloud or in your head, repeat your chosen mantra.

3. Do this for a few minutes, noticing the waves of calmness that flow through you. When you're ready, think about someone you love and care for: a lover, a close friend, a family member. Think about them, picturing them in your mind's eye. Take that warm glow you've been holding and send it out towards them. As you do so, repeat your mantra, but this time instead of 'May I', say 'May [the person's name]'.

4. As you repeat these words, really focus on sending that sense of love and compassion out to this person.

5. After a few minutes, move on to the next stage. Think of someone you don't feel too fond of. It could be your school bully, a domineering person at work, or an ex-friend or old partner who you don't particularly like. When you're ready, repeat the mantra using their name, and send love and compassion out to them.

6. This kind of practice can help us let go of feelings of bitterness and resentment, and also promotes wellbeing and more compassionate behaviour towards others.

JOURNAL PROMPT: LOVE LETTER

✳

One of the most important aspects of a healthy Heart Chakra is the ability to love yourself. It's not something that comes naturally to all of us, so this journal prompt might be quite challenging. You may have to try it more than once before you feel comfortable.

Sit down with your journal and compose a love letter to yourself. Tell yourself the things you really love and admire about yourself: the things you're proud of, the things you think make you a good person. They can be abstract – perhaps you're patient or generous or optimistic – or more tangible – perhaps you have beautiful eyes or a lovely singing voice. You don't have to use the kind of flowery, poetic language we often associate with love letters. You just have to be genuine. Try to move past any feelings of self-consciousness or self-doubt that come up, and just focus on the words you are putting on the page.

When you're finished, keep the letter somewhere safe and return to it from time to time to remind yourself what a special person you are.

THE THROAT
CHAKRA

Sanskrit: *Vishuddha*, meaning 'purification'

Colour: Turquoise/light blue

Element: Spirit/ether

Symbol: Sixteen-petalled lotus containing an inverted triangle and a circle

Key words: Communication, expression, voice

The Throat Chakra is all about communication and self-expression. Our ability to communicate effectively can have a huge impact on our sense of wellbeing. If we're able to share our thoughts, feeling and opinions, to make ourselves understood, and to ask for help or support when we need it, we feel happier, calmer and safer.

The voice is a powerful tool. It can be used to express kindness, share truth and connect with others, but it can also be used to cause harm – to spread lies, to create distrust, to hurt or offend others. Because of this power, it's a tool we have to use with care, and an important part of this can be the Throat Chakra.

When your Throat Chakra is unblocked and allowing energy to flow as it should, you will be able to express yourself freely and clearly. Your words will flow with ease, and you will speak at a natural, easy pace and volume, making you someone other people enjoy talking with. You will use your voice for the expression of truth, not for causing harm or for idle gossip. You may not talk a lot, but when you do speak, your words will be thoughtful and eloquent, spoken with integrity and kindness.

Although the Throat Chakra's position means we automatically associate it with verbal communication, you may express yourself in other ways – for example through writing, art or music. Even if the message isn't coming out of your mouth, the expression of it is still linked to the Throat Chakra.

Because communication is a two-way street, the Throat Chakra is also concerned with listening. When your Throat Chakra is functioning properly, you will be able to listen to others with care and consideration, and people will feel able to come to you and share their thoughts without inhibition or uncertainty.

HOW CAN YOU TELL IF YOUR THROAT CHAKRA IS DAMAGED OR WEAKENED?

If your Throat Chakra is damaged or weakened, you might struggle to communicate effectively. You may be quite timid or shy, reluctant to speak up in a group situation or horrified by the thought of public speaking.

A common problem with a weakened Throat Chakra is a fear of confrontation. If you are struggling with a blockage or weakness in this chakra, you may find you will go to great lengths to avoid confrontation: perhaps you would rather eat the wrong meal in a restaurant than ask the waiter to take it back; perhaps the thought of saying no to your boss is so uncomfortable that you stay late when asked even if you had other plans; perhaps you can't bring yourself to express your disappointment to your partner when they do something you wish they hadn't.

You may also find that people interrupt you or speak over you a lot. In lively debates or energetic back-and-forth conversations between groups of friends, it's not unusual for people to get overexcited and all speak at once, but if you find your voice consistently gets buried by those of others, it's a good indication that this chakra needs some help.

Not expressing yourself and leaving words unsaid can leave you with a sense of burden, as you're carrying thoughts and feelings around with you with no way of sharing them with others or getting rid of them. This heavy feeling can really weigh you down, and may lead to feelings of hopelessness or despair. You might find it so hard to express yourself to others that you aren't even honest with yourself,

> **An overactive Throat Chakra can see you talking too much, too fast or too loudly.**

avoiding thinking about difficult subjects or burying your feelings when they do come up. This can give you a strange sense of being somehow disconnected from your body.

HOW CAN YOU TELL IF YOUR THROAT CHAKRA IS OVERACTIVE?

An overactive Throat Chakra can see you talking too much, too fast or too loudly. You might speak without really thinking first, starting a sentence without actually knowing how you intend to finish it.

You may have a tendency to speak over others, interrupting them and dominating the conversation. Listening is such an important skill, and an overactive Throat Chakra can mean you end up not really listening, but rather waiting for the other person to stop speaking so that it will be your turn to talk again. You may also be prone to repeating yourself, telling the same stories over and over.

Sometimes, people who communicate in this way feel like they're being gregarious and outgoing, but it can actually make you a very draining and challenging person to be around. Other people may find it frustrating that you interrupt, take over conversations and fail to listen. They may actually avoid telling you things because they think you won't listen anyway.

Another significant issue with an overactive Throat Chakra is best summed up by the phrase 'All mouth and no trousers'. In other words, if the Throat Chakra is spinning at such a pace that it's taking in all the energy, it can prevent energy from flowing up or down to the other chakras. This can cause situations like someone coming up with a brilliant idea thanks to energy in their higher chakras, but not being able to put

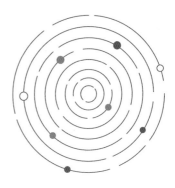

it into action because the energy gets tangled up in the Throat Chakra rather than travelling down to the more practical lower chakras: so essentially, the person just talks incessantly about their idea without doing anything about it. It can happen the other way, too – for example, someone experiencing challenges due to discomforts felt in their lower chakras may complain endlessly to others rather than allowing the energy to flow up to the higher chakras where ideas for solutions might be created.

HOW TO CARE FOR YOUR THROAT CHAKRA

A healthy Throat Chakra allows you to express yourself and share experiences, thoughts and feelings with those around you. Bringing balance to this vital and powerful chakra can create new opportunities and enhance your relationships.

BREATHING EXERCISES

Most breathing exercises can be used to strengthen the Throat Chakra, as the flow of air through the physical throat can echo the flow of energy through the chakra.

A very simple exercise is to sit or stand upright, with your feet firmly planted on the floor. Take a long, deep breath in through your nose. As the breath enters your body, try to follow it down your throat and into your lungs. Imagine it flooding you with a cool, calming blue light. Pause for a moment, then forcibly exhale through your mouth, forcing the air out with a powerful sigh. Repeat a couple more times.

READ ALOUD

If speaking up can be challenging for you, try reading aloud to yourself in order to get used to using your voice. Aim to spend about 10 minutes a day on this. Take the time to read in a steady and measured voice, and pay attention to your breathing and pacing so that the words don't all rush together in a garbled muddle. As you become more comfortable with your own voice, you will find it easier to speak aloud in other situations.

NECK MASSAGE

We don't need much encouragement to go for a massage anyway, but a luxurious neck massage can work wonders for your Throat Chakra, lavishing attention on the area, loosening knots and aches, and opening up the space so that your chakra can function at is best.

CAT-COW

One of the most basic yoga poses, cat-cow is a simple but powerful movement that engages the whole spine and can help to unblock or ease the Throat Chakra.

Begin on all fours, with your spine neutral. As you inhale, move into 'cow' pose: gently arch your back, lifting your tail bone upwards,

✴

The colours associated with the Throat Chakra are turquoise and light blue: calming, peaceful colours that are soothing to be around.

✴

> **On bright, sunny days, take a moment to fling your head back and enjoy the dizzying blue of the sky.**

lifting your chest, and softly stretching your neck so that your eyes are looking upwards.

BASK IN BLUE

The colours associated with the Throat Chakra are turquoise and light blue: calming, peaceful colours that are soothing to be around. Look for ways to bring them into your day. A great option is to wear a tie or a necklace in these colours, as its physical position around your throat serves as a double reminder to keep this chakra cared for and balanced. Look for blue flowers to brighten up your space, and try drinking from blue-coloured glasses or other vessels. On bright, sunny days, take a moment to fling your head back and enjoy the dizzying blue of the sky, or seek out bodies of water that will reflect the blue above.

JOURNAL TO BECOME USED TO EXPRESSING YOURSELF

Journaling is useful for all the chakras, and we've given a particular journal prompt at the end of the chapter, but journaling in general is a really valuable tool if you're struggling with weakness or damage to your Throat Chakra. Speaking up can be challenging, but journaling allows you to practise expressing yourself in a more private and low-key space. You might find that journaling about a particular issue, such as a relationship problem or a work challenge, helps you to get clear in your mind about how you feel and what you would like to communicate, so when the time comes, you are better able to put your point across.

CHALLENGE YOURSELF TO SAY ONE THING IN EACH MEETING

If you've always found speaking up in work meetings to be nerve-wracking, then the idea of launching head-on into a discussion might seem impossible. Instead, make a quiet deal with yourself that you'll say at least one thing in each meeting from now on. It doesn't have to be big; it could be saying, 'I agree,' or 'That would work really well' when somebody else says something you agree with. Doing this will help you to become used to speaking up without rushing yourself into a situation you're not ready for, and it will also help your colleagues get used to hearing from you. Over time, they'll naturally start drawing you into the discussions more, as you are demonstrating a willingness to participate.

SAY, 'I HADN'T FINISHED SPEAKING'

This can be really difficult, and may not be something you can manage early on in your Throat Chakra work, but if you find that others speak over you a lot, there is nothing wrong with calmly and kindly saying, 'I hadn't quite finished with what I wanted to say.' The person who interrupted you might be a bit embarrassed, but it's unlikely that they spoke over you maliciously, and they will probably apologize and invite you to continue. Because it's often easier to stand up for others than ourselves, you might find you prefer to speak up when you notice someone else getting interrupted. When the person who did the interrupting has finished or paused, try turning to the original speaker and inviting them to continue. If you don't want to come straight out and mention they were interrupted, you could try saying something

like, 'I didn't catch all of what you said, do you mind going over it again?' Modelling this type of behaviour encourages those around us to be more thoughtful about their own communication styles, and you may find there are fewer interruptions, or that others invite you to finish when the same thing happens to you.

IF YOUR THROAT CHAKRA IS OVERACTIVE

If you have an overeager Throat Chakra and just can't seem to stop yourself from gabbling on, make a concerted effort to practise active listening. Active listening is exactly what it sounds like: listening with your full attention and focus, really absorbing what the other person is saying, and – crucially – not reacting to it verbally until they have definitely finished. You can show you are listening by nodding or making gently encouraging noises like

'Hmm' and 'Uh huh', but don't let this become distracting. Give the other person the floor and let them say what they need to.

Another useful skill for calming down the Throat Chakra is to make a point of thinking about what you're going to say before speaking. In high-pressure situations, such as job interviews, it can be all too easy to launch into a speech or response without really thinking about where we're going. This can leave us meandering, chattering aimlessly or even tailing off awkwardly when we run out of steam. Take a moment, force yourself to take a breath and think, and then, once you know what you want to say, speak.

Bringing balance to this vital and powerful chakra can create new opportunities and enhance your relationships.

MEDITATION: MANTRAS AND HUMMING

A simple meditation for the Throat Chakra is to make use of mantras or humming. If you would like to use a mantra, think of one before you begin. It might be one that relates specifically to your Throat Chakra struggles, for example, 'I will use my voice.'

1. Sit in a calm, quiet space where you can be uninterrupted for 10-15 minutes. Sit in a chair or on the floor with your spine straight and a neutral expression on your face. Breathe in and out slowly and allow a sense of calm to settle over you. When you're ready, begin to repeat your mantra aloud, speaking slowly and clearly. If you prefer, you can hum instead, feeling the vibrations in your throat and focusing on the feeling of openness and potential there.

JOURNAL PROMPT: UNSPOKEN WORDS

Think of a time when you didn't speak up, even though there was something you wanted or need to express. This could be something that happened when you were a child, or something more recent. Often, these situations come with a sense of unfairness or injustice. You might wish you had felt able to stand up for yourself. Or perhaps there was a moment when you wanted to tell someone you were in love with how you felt about them, but you couldn't make the words come out.

How did it feel, in that moment? Were the words caught in your throat, your mouth, or elsewhere? What would you have said if you could?

What would it have felt like to express these feelings aloud?

THE THIRD
EYE CHAKRA

Sanskrit: *Ajna*, meaning 'command'

Colour: Indigo or deep blue

Element: Spirit/cosmic energy

Symbol: Two-petalled diamond-shaped lotus

Key words: Intuition, awareness perspective, clarity

As we journey through the chakras, we are now in the higher, more spiritual chakras. Everything here is a little more abstract, a little more nuanced. The Third Eye Chakra or Brow Chakra is concerned with wisdom, understanding and wider knowledge. It's about intuition, but unlike the 'gut feeling' intuition associated with the Solar Plexus Chakra (see page 58), this is about a sense of wisdom and knowing. Some people associate the Third Eye Chakra with clairvoyance and telepathy. If this isn't your thing, it still has strong links with perception, intellect and seeing things differently.

If your Third Eye Chakra is balanced and functioning well, you will have a sense of clarity and awareness in your life. You will be inspired and creative, yet logical and practical. You know that sense of calm efficiency that we get when everything is going according to plan? This is like that, on a soul level. It's a sense of knowing, and seeing, and being at ease with what is.

You will have a gift for seeing things as they really are, without getting distracted by other people's opinions, demands and desires. You'll be able to look beyond the obvious. You'll have a strong sense of what really matters, and a firm grasp on your own values.

You'll be an effective and creative problem-solver, and you might sometimes spot solutions and patterns that others miss. You have a sense that there is more to life beyond the material, physical world, but you use this knowledge to enhance your experiences and interactions in the physical world.

HOW CAN YOU TELL IF YOUR THIRD EYE CHAKRA IS DAMAGED OR WEAKENED?

If your Third Eye Chakra is blocked or not functioning as it should, you will be rather narrow-minded: not great at seeing the bigger picture. You won't be good at picking up on nuance, and you may struggle with things that require use of imagination – things like reading fiction or poetry, or abstract art.

Your friends would probably describe you as grounded, and that's not a bad way to be – as we saw in earlier chapters, being grounded can be a sign of healthy lower chakras – but you may have a sense that something isn't quite right – that there should be more to life. This might come up as dissatisfaction or frustration, because you're trying to find a practical solution for a problem that isn't really tangible.

It's worth remembering that spending too much time in front of screens or in crowded, overstimulating environments can be damaging to the Third Eye Chakra – so day-to-day life in the modern world, with all its scrolling and notifications and noise, can cause a lot of issues for this chakra.

HOW CAN YOU TELL IF YOUR THIRD EYE CHAKRA IS OVERACTIVE?

If your Third Eye Chakra is overactive, you might be quite superstitious and sometimes even prone to paranoia. Your friends might affectionately say that your head is in the clouds, and it's likely you struggle with the practical aspects of life.

You may often feel overwhelmed and overstimulated, and out of touch with reality. Your overactive imagination and tendency to absorb everything about your surroundings may mean you often struggle with concentration.

You might feel like your mind is clouded and too full, and you've been known to jump to conclusions. You could also be prone to worrying about the future, thanks in part to that very busy imagination of yours.

Everything here is a little more abstract, a little more nuanced.

HOW TO CARE FOR YOUR THIRD EYE CHAKRA

A healthy Third Eye Chakra allows you to approach life with a sense of calm curiosity and welcome. Finding ways to care for and balance this intuitive and intellectual chakra can leave you filled with wisdom and understanding.

LEARN TO TRUST YOUR INTUITION

If you don't trust your intuition, you don't give it a chance to strengthen and develop. The next time you have to make a decision, however big or small, pause for a moment and try to feel what's happening, both in your physical body and your energetic one. You might feel that familiar settling sensation in your stomach area – the 'gut feeling' we talked about on page 101. Try to feel beyond that and get a wider sense for the decision you're trying to make. Consider the options and pay close attention. Is there, however subtle, a sense of

'rightness' or 'wrongness' that you can detect? Try not to look directly at it, but instead allow it to come to you and settle in your mind. Give yourself space and permission to trust it.

DREAM DIARY

The subconscious and the Third Eye Chakra are closely linked, so paying attention to your dreams can be a powerful way to gain a better connection with this chakra. Often, we dream about things that our subconscious mind is trying to understand or resolve, but it may use abstract images and symbols as it does this. Try keeping a dream diary. Keep a notebook next to your bed and, as soon as you wake up or remember a snippet of a dream, write it down. Try to include all the details you can remember – colours, shapes and general feelings can all take on new meaning and importance later on. As your Third Eye Chakra strengthens, you may start to spot patterns and meanings in your dreams.

PAY ATTENTION TO COINCIDENCES

Have you ever been thinking about someone and then bumped into them unexpectedly? Or walked into a second-hand bookshop only to spot the very book you've been thinking about all week? Sometimes, of course, coincidences are just that and nothing more, but by paying attention to them, we become better at spotting patterns and getting a sense for when and how things may happen.

*

As your Third Eye Chakra strengthens, you may start to spot patterns and meanings in your dreams.

*

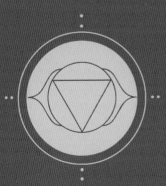

...hone your ability to see beyond what's right in front of you.

PRACTISE VISUALIZING

If you struggle to imagine or visualize things that aren't directly in front of you, try reading a descriptive scene from a book or short story, then close your eyes and try to 'see' the scene unfold in front of you. Populate the image in your mind with the characters. If the writing gave visual clues as to their appearances, then include those in your visualization; if not, come up with your own. Try to include and imagine as much detail as possible.

PICK UP PURPLE

Incorporate dark blues and deep purples into your day-to-day life as a visual cue to focus on your Third Eye Chakra. Try wearing purple eyeshadow or eyeliner, or adding a dash of indigo to your outfit in some other way. Blueberries are a great food to support this chakra – as well as being deliciously purple, they are full of antioxidants that are helpful for brain health. Purple flowers or home furnishings can also remind you to make space for this chakra in your life.

SEEK OUT PATTERNS

Looking for patterns and shapes within other items can help strengthen your Third Eye Chakra and hone your ability to see beyond what's right in front of you. A common way to do this is with clouds, by gazing up at the sky and allowing your mind to notice different patterns and shapes within their fluffy forms. You can also do it with patterned wallpaper, woodgrain, smoke, patches of moss or lichen, and open fires or candles.

FACTOR IN TIME FOR MEDITATION AND SPIRITUAL PURSUITS

Because the Third Eye Chakra is a more abstract and spiritual chakra, simply carving out time for things like meditation, mindfulness and spiritual reading will give you the best possible chance at strengthening and balancing this chakra. It can be hard to find the time for these things when we're busy, but there is a popular – and accurate – adage in Zen Buddhism that says, 'If you're too busy to meditate for one hour, you should meditate for two hours.' In other words, if you're too busy to make time for the things that will help your body and soul, you need those things even more.

IF YOUR THIRD EYE CHAKRA IS OVERACTIVE

Because the chakras are all about balance, if your upper chakras are overactive, you can try to balance them by strengthening your lowers ones. Try the exercises under 'How to care for your Base Chakra' on page 34.

MEDITATION: SEEING BEYOND SIGHT

As always, read this meditation through before you begin.

1. Sit in a calm, quiet place where you won't be disturbed for about 20 minutes. Sit upright on a chair, with your feet planted on the ground and your spine straight. Make sure you're comfortable, relaxed and supported.

2. Close your eyes and breath slowly and steadily, in and out. Now focus your attention on the spot between your eyebrows, where your Third Eye Chakra is located. As you breathe, imagine all your energy and intention moving into this space. Imagine a deep blue or indigo light emanating from your brow. As this light shines in front of you, imagine it illuminating what is there, and all the layers beneath it. Imagine this connecting you to the past, present and future – to something beyond the here and now. Allow the glow to reach out and spread, emanating from your brow, and sit and breathe in harmony with this glow.

3. When you're ready, pull your focus back to your physical body, paying special attention to your legs and feet to help ground you once more.

JOURNAL PROMPT: INTUITION

As you learn to pay attention to and trust your intuition, journaling can be an effective tool. Think about a time when you felt a strong intuitive sense about something – perhaps you felt sure that someone's plan wasn't going to work, but you couldn't entirely put a finger on why. Or maybe you had a feeling that a situation was going to play out in a particular way, although you had no way of knowing. Write about it: about what you thought would happen, and how the intuition felt, both physically and spiritually. Now write about what actually happened. Was your intuition correct? Or if it wasn't, think about what might have clouded it. This exercise will help you find clarity and trust in your 'sixth sense'.

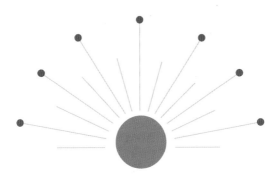

THE CROWN CHAKRA

Sanskrit: *Sahasrara*, meaning 'thousand petals'

Colour: Violet/white/gold

Element: Spirit/cosmic energy

Symbol: Thousand-petalled lotus

Key words: Spirituality, divinity, wonder, unity

The Crown Chakra is an abstract and ethereal chakra that is hard to define. It is about inner wisdom, but also extends to a sort of universal consciousness. With this chakra we are moving beyond the body and reaching upwards and outwards to connect on a higher level.

When the Crown Chakra is balanced and working optimally, you will feel balanced. You will feel calm, spiritually satisfied, and at ease with the universe and your place in it. If you believe in a god, deity or spiritual being, you may feel a sense of divine connection;

if not, you may experience more of a sense of connection and oneness with the universe.

You will have a sense of a higher or divine purpose, and you will feel great trust in the universe, which can be immensely comforting. You will be aware of the patterns and connections occurring all around you, and move through life with an air of serenity, compassion and unity.

HOW CAN YOU TELL IF YOUR CROWN CHAKRA IS DAMAGED OR WEAKENED?

If your Crown Chakra is damaged or weakened, you will be lacking that sense of intense connection we discussed in the previous chapter. Instead, you may feel somewhat lonely and detached, as though you are somehow separate from everything else.

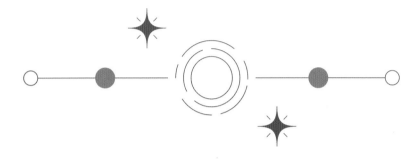

You might feel almost as if the rest of the world is on one side of a pane of glass and you are on the other, unable to reach through. You may feel uninspired, listless, fidgety and bored; you might seek constant distraction in an effort to soothe your sense of dissatisfaction, but physical and material objects and activities cannot satisfy this need.

If your Crown Chakra is weakened or blocked but your lower chakras are functioning well, it's entirely possible to live a life that appears, from the outside at least, to be successful: you may have material wealth, social power and connections, and loving relationships – but you might sometimes get a slight sense that something is missing, or isn't quite aligned. Perhaps you're not sure of your purpose in life, or what it all means. If you examine this feeling more closely, you may find it can be linked back to your Crown Chakra.

HOW CAN YOU TELL IF YOUR CROWN CHAKRA IS OVERACTIVE?

An overactive Crown Chakra can have a similar impact to an overactive Third Eye Chakra (see page 103), but with everything being a little more intense. If your Crown Chakra is overactive, you may have a loose grip on reality that makes living in the real world deeply challenging. You might be prone to disappearing into yourself. You may fail to take adequate care of your physical health because you don't feel a connection with your body.

You may be vulnerable to extreme ideologies and fanaticism, as you reach further and further into abstract concepts and philosophies without retaining a grasp of their real-world impacts.

✳

An overactive Crown Chakra can have a similar impact to an overactive Third Eye Chakra.

✳

HOW TO CARE FOR YOUR CROWN CHAKRA

A healthy Crown Chakra gives you the opportunity to live a truly fulfilling life. Although accessing very high levels of spiritual attunement may not be possible for most people, finding ways to care for and balance this most profound of chakras can bring you tranquillity and deep, deep joy.

HEAD MASSAGE

Book yourself a beautiful head massage with aromatic oils and soothing lighting. Allow the touch of the massage therapist's fingers to invigorate and soothe you, helping to open your Crown Chakra and fill you with calm and purpose.

LOOK FOR VIOLET, WHITE AND GOLD

The Crown Chakra is at the very edge of the rainbow colour spectrum, a shimmering haze that emerges from violet to ethereal white to glittering gold. Seek out these rich, powerful colours and bathe in their beauty. Try wearing a gold necklace or ring set with an amethyst or an opalescent white moonstone as a reminder to focus on the Crown Chakra. Try eating white, airy foods, like whipped up meringues, light-as-air panna cotta or even melt-in-the-mouth white candy floss. Spending time with these peaceful, spiritual colours will help to activate the Crown Chakra and strengthen your connection with it.

SEEK OUT
THE SUBLIME

When we talked about the Base Chakra, we spoke about getting outside into nature (see page 34), but as well as being deeply grounding, nature can be utterly awe-inspiring. Seek out dizzying mountain tops, dazzling underground caves, jewel-toned forest glades and stormy seafronts. Take a moment to stand in wonder, connecting with the sublime and revelling in the exquisite and expansive beauty of the world around you.

✦ **Make time every day to stop and be still. No headphones, no screens, no distractions.** ✦

TAKE TIME FOR STILLNESS

Make time every day to stop and be still. No headphones, no screens, no distractions. Just sit in awareness of your own existence, listening to the hum of the world around you as the universe breathes and moves through its endless cycles.

IF YOUR CROWN CHAKRA IS OVERACTIVE

As with the Third Eye Chakra, grounding exercises are an excellent way to balance the Crown Chakra - see pages 41–43. You may also like to explore the exercises for the Sacral Chakra on page 55, as this can give you a greater sense of belonging within your own body when you are feeling somewhat detached.

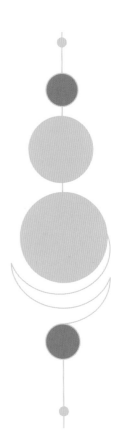

MEDITATION: ZOOMING OUT

✳

This meditation uses a visualization to help you imagine the sheer scope and scale of the universe. Read it all the way through before you begin. If you like, you could record yourself reading it aloud and then listen to the recording as you meditate.

1. As always, sit in a calm, quiet space where you won't be disturbed for about 20 minutes. Make sure you're comfortable, and sit on a chair with your feet firmly placed on the ground. Breathe slowly in and out for a few minutes.

2. Move your attention to the top of your head, to the location of the Crown Chakra. Imagine a glowing ball of light, shimmering in those gold, white and violet tones. Now imagine the light slowly rising, up and away from your head. Allow it to move through the ceiling, through the floors above, through the roof, and outside. Let it continue to rise, up beyond the building, over the trees, towards the birds and clouds and sky. Below, the world recedes: buildings and cars look like toys; streets and rivers become fine lines. Continue to rise, following the light up and up into the atmosphere and out into space.

3. The Earth is below, a green and blue orb wreathed in white clouds. Rise and expand further and further, through the stars, beyond the Milky Way, into the cosmos, surrounded by the swirls of galaxies and the epic vastness of the universe.

4. Breathe in and feel the gold-white-violet light connecting you with all of this.

5. When you're ready, slowly pull your focus towards your feet, still resting securely on the ground, so far below. Slowly move back through the layers you rose through – the galaxies, the solar system, the Earth's atmosphere, the clouds, the sky, the building, the ceiling – until your focus is firmly back on the ground, but with a sense still of that wonderful connection. Spend some time slowly breathing here to fully ground yourself.

JOURNAL PROMPT: SPIRITUALITY

Spirituality is an abstract and subjective concept that means different things to different people. Write about what spirituality means to you. Does it pertain to religion, to the natural world, to some cosmic unknown? Is it about a deeper connection within yourself? Where do you find spirituality in your daily life – through music, art, nature, love? Explore these ideas and feelings to crystallize your own understanding of spirituality and help you better understand the concept of the Crown Chakra.

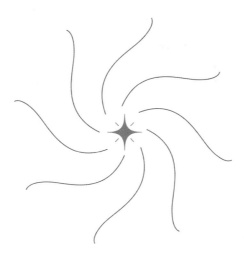

FULL-BODY CHAKRA SCAN

Now that we've explored each of the chakras in depth, and you have an idea of their functions and the effects they can have on your day-to-day life, this final exercise draws on the idea of the body-scan meditation, often used in mindfulness practices, incorporating the chakras into the experience.

Read this through in full before you begin. If you prefer, you can record yourself reading it aloud and then listen to the recording as you meditate.

Find a warm, calm, comfortable quiet space where you can be left undisturbed for about 20 minutes. Lie down, either on the floor, on a yoga mat or on a sofa or bed. Just make sure you have space to lie on your back, with your arms resting at your sides and your legs fully extended. Make sure you're comfortable and that your spine is straight and well-supported.

Breathing slowly and deeply, with calm, measured inhales and exhales, slowly allow any tension you're holding in your body to drift away. Become aware of how it feels to be in your body. Notice where parts of your body are touching the surface on which you're lying. Take a few minutes here.

We'll begin with the Base Chakra. When you're ready, turn your attention to your feet, focusing on how they feel – your toes, the soles of your feet. Notice if you have any pain or tension there. Try to relax them as much as you can. As you do this, allow the attention you are focusing on your feet to glow with the red of the Base Chakra. Think about the way your feet ground you and connect you to the earth. Slowly allow the red glow to move up your legs, to your calves, knees, thighs, then your hips. As you go, continue to notice any pain, discomfort or tension, and if you find any, try to shine the red glow on to it to help dissipate it. Move up past your groin to the base of your spine, where the Base Chakra sits. Focus here for a while, letting the red glow emanate out from the Base Chakra to the rest of your body. If you feel any discomfort or uncertainty, try to turn the red glow towards it. Allow a sense of safety and security to settle around you, helping you feel sheltered, nourished and at ease.

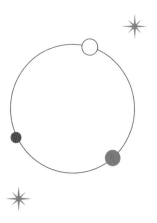

When you're ready, move on to the Sacral Chakra. Slowly allow your focus to move up the spine to the Sacral Chakra, just below the navel. As you do so, let the glow change from red to orange. Let the orange glow shine out from the Sacral Chakra, spreading a sense of joy and delight. Focus on the pleasant feelings in your body: warmth, comfort, relaxation. Notice the soft fabric of your clothes or the feel of the surface beneath you. If you are feeling tired or dissatisfied, or

uncomfortable in your own body, try to focus on that soft, warm orange glow and the joy contained within it, letting its sensual energy flow through you.

Next, move on to the Solar Plexus Chakra. Gradually move your focus further up the spine to the Solar Plexus Chakra, above the navel and below the sternum. As you do so, imagine the glow changing from orange to a sunny yellow. Feel it begin to buzz with power and potential, and allow that sense of power and control to move through your body, emanating out from the Solar Plexus Chakra. If you notice feelings of discomfort in your gut or a sense of nervousness or weakness, bring your focus to them and bathe them in the yellow glow of the Solar Plexus Chakra, bringing you confidence and positivity.

Now we move further up the spine to the Heart Chakra, in the centre of the chest. As you move your focus here, let the glow change from yellow to green. Breathe here for a few moments, letting feelings of love, compassion and kindness flow through the Heart Chakra. If you notice any feelings of being blocked or resistant, gently shine the green glow towards them and help them ease and fade. Allow a sense of gratitude and peace to settle around you as your being fills with love.

Although the chakras can be deeply spiritual, they also have their place in everyday life.

Breathe deeply as we progress up the spine to the Throat Chakra. As the glow travels upwards, let its colour change from green to light blue or turquoise, spreading a soothing aqua light through the body. Focus your attention on the throat and the power of your own voice, your ability to communicate and express yourself with integrity and clarity. If you notice any sense of feeling blocked or tongue-tied, try to shine that blue glow towards these feelings to help them fade.

Now we move on to the Third Eye Chakra. Move your focus up to your brow, letting the glow change in colour from blue to a deep indigo. Pull all your attention towards this spot, imagining the purple glow flowing out. Try to draw on any sense of wisdom, certainty or intuition you can feel. Let your mind and body respond to the feeling of knowing, with clarity and calm moving through you. If you feel any resistance here,

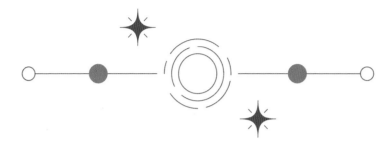

or a sense of dissatisfaction or disconnection, shine that purple glowing light towards it, trying to ease these feelings with a sense of knowledge and connection.

And finally, let the glow travel up to the top of your head and the Crown Chakra. As it moves, let the colour change from deep indigo to a shimmering violet with white and gold accents. As this ethereal light glows out from your Crown Chakra, reach for feelings of serenity, peace and cosmic connection. If you notice feelings of boredom or detachment, shine the light on them with a sense of compassion and trust in the universe.

Stay here for a few moments, then, with a push of joyful energy, imagine each of the chakras lighting up with its corresponding colour, and imagine the glow of each one flowing easily up and down the spine, reaching into the rest of your body and being, in perfect, tranquil harmony.

Spend some time here with the rainbow glow of your chakras, enjoying the experience of balance and connection. When you're ready, slowly bring your focus back to the feeling of your body lying on the surface.

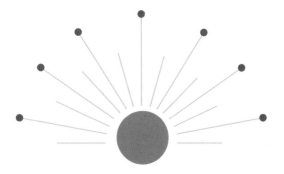

Breathe in and out, really feeling your lungs and the way the air enters and exits your body. After a few moments, open your eyes and slowly bring yourself back into the room.

Try to carry this sense of balance and energy with you throughout the day.

CONCLUSION

We hope this book has shown you that although the chakras can be deeply spiritual, they also have their place in everyday life. Caring for each one encourages habits and behaviours that are beneficial to you in different areas of your life, from your most basic needs, to enhanced relationships with those you love, to fulfilment in your intellectual and spiritual experiences. Paying attention to our chakras and their energy helps us understand when and how things are going wrong in our lives, especially as the real issue isn't always easy to identify.

With time, patience and self-compassion, you can work on your chakras to bring a sense of balance, harmony and positive energy to every day.

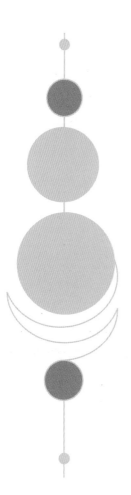

Spend some time
with the rainbow
glow of your
chakras, enjoying
the experience
of balance and
connection.